PROUD GODS AND COMMODORES

PROUD GODS AND COMMODORES

ASSORTED POEMS AND EPIC TALES
(Volume 1)

JAMES MCMILLAN

Copyright © 2021 by James McMillan

All rights reserved. No part of this publication may be reproduced, distributed, or transmitted in any form or by any means, including photocopying, recording, or other electronic or mechanical methods without the prior written permission of the publisher. For permission requests, solicit the publisher via the address below through mail or email with the subject line "Attention: Publication Permission".

This publication contains the opinions and ideas of its author. It is intended to provide helpful and informative material on the subjects addressed in the publication. The author and publisher specifically disclaim all responsibility for any liability, loss, or risk, personal or otherwise, which is incurred as a consequence, directly or indirectly, of the use and application of any of the contents of this book.

Dedication

This book is dedicated first of all to Doctor Minghelli Lieu, right here in Modesto, cardiovascular surgeon, without whom not only would there be no book, but also no me as well. No bullshit, Dr. Lieu… no bullshit.

Also my deepest respect and heartfelt appreciation to all the nurses and staff of the cardiovascular intensive care unit, Doctors Hospital, Modesto California. Each of you for me was like a hand of God.

My special thanks to John the nurse, big guy, 60 years old, gray beard, reminded me of Santa Claus, who when I awoke from that heart attack, no idea where I was or what had happened, what seemed a shotgun wound in my chest, tubes and ducts running in and out of me, bags of liquids dangling over me like a chorus of told-you-so's, and John looked down on me and said, "Doc, you were not on the train to Oblivion, but you were sure standing on the platform." Thanks, John, from all my heart still beating and thumping because of you and the others, encouraging me and inspiring me even when I thought nothing left in the tank.

Also, I want to give special shout-out and grateful thanks to everyone at Cardiac Rehab downtown Modesto, your helping me and encouraging me.

    Wayne Cheung
    Nicole Wilson
    Samantha Samra
    Felix Soto
    Mikaela Delacruz

Every one of you is a saint to me and always will be to the end of my days.

God bless you all.

PROUD GODS AND COMMODORES II

"God is dead."—

A phrase echoing today throughout the hallowed halls and corridors of Academia, a concept lifted from the works of the philosopher Frederick Nietzsche, he who also created the concept of the SuperMan, Ubermensch, an idea seized and exploited eagerly by Nazis and triggering unspeakable horror world-wide upon the earth. Is it possible concepts are like people— defined by the company they keep, and therefore to have one is surely to have the other?

"But delights to him, who against the proud gods and commodores of this earth, stands forth his own inexorable self— who condemns all sin, though he pluck it out from under the robes of Senators and Judges. And eternal delights shall be his who coming to lay him down can say, "Oh Father, mortal or immortal here I die. I've striven to be thine more than this world's or mine own. Yet this is nothing. I leave eternity to thee, for what is man if he should live out the lifetime of his God."—
— Father Mapple (<u>Moby Dick</u>)

Author's Note

When I was young I ran with San Francisco's counter-culture revolutionaries, wanting to burn it all down, even a trek to Cuba for a radical meeting with Fidel, cutting sugar cane with him, then at dinner all of us eagerly listening to his self-serving yet sometimes rhapsodic even humorous exhortations on "El Pueblo" and revolution, unleashing within us that 'Ubermensch Derangement Syndrome,' that your humanity is somehow greater than another's humanity, therefore empowering you over them, including of course a lynch mob if necessary.

Later because of injury I virtually fell into Chiropractic college, a Damascus experience, Saul to Paul.

Though this book is not about Chiropractic at all, it does reflect the profound change its holistic study and philosophy inspired in me.

What an adjustment is to the body,
a good poem is to the soul.

A number of poems in this collection are what's called 'maguffins,' which is an old Alfred Hitchcock term for plot devices, that is hinges upon which the plot swings but really themselves are not essential to the story.

A classic example is the stolen money in "Psycho," or the gold or whatever it is in the briefcase of "Pulp Fiction," or even one could say the blackbird itself in the movie "Maltese Falcon," or The Memphis Belle in "Memphis Belle," all just devices to evolve the characters and move the story, yet in themselves are not really essential to the story, or especially to character resolution, just devices to keep things moving along, as opposed to HAL in "2001," a villain at the time when society was paranoid about computers, but 30 years into it, the computer age, HAL redeems himself in "2010," itself a disappointing and pretentious film in which HAL's redemption, courage and self-sacrifice are the most interesting, most noble, and by far the most moving of all the human interactions of that film,…just saying.

Several poems in this collection, especially the first, 'The Rape of Athena,' and *all* of the tales are exactly that— maguffins— their ostensibly written by various characters in the two epic sagas I am currently writing, as well as the several excerpts in these volumes taken directly from those sagas:

**The Journal of Taranis the Helvetian,
the Man Who Loves Wild RedCat Woman,
Kazhana the Akatani**

and

**HighPockets and the Blue Guitar,
Searching for the Face of God**

I know, I know, those titles sound pretentious, but you'll just have to thank my middle son for that. Besides who of us is not pretentious whenever the moment is right... not you, mom!

So, the maguffins in this collection are so marked and noted. The rest are all my own poems and gnarly Haiku, pretty much in chronological order. I hope you find some you like.

One last thing, at the end of both the first and second volume I'm including the introduction and prefaces to those two sagas I'm writing. My hope is that all this is a teaser to whet your appetite for them. We shall see.

Jim McMillan

TABLE OF CONTENTS

SELECTED POEMS:

The Rape Of Athena 1
Rationalist Lament 25
To Be or Not To Be 25
Poor Man's Dilemna 26
God Bless Ben Franklin 26
Sound of Hope 26
Gaining Consciousness 27
Warrior 27
Singing Blues with My Father 28
Oberón's Variati on on a Theme by Dylan 33
For Oberón: Another variation on a Theme by Dylan (Sarah) 35
Miss Mary Madelin's Creed 36
Healer's Dilemna 37
Hot Summer Day 37
Malagueña Faerie Queen 39
Widow's Ta ke on Tennessee Willia ms 40
Portrait of Jennie, a Movie, 1953 40
Be Thou Still in the Moonlight 41
Chapultapec (Los Niños Heroes) 42
A Nod to Pogo and Mahatma 42
Quote in Starbuck's 43
Penitent Man 44
I Would Love You Better Now 45
Sunrise Prayer 45
Smooch, the Fat Feline, Neglected 46
Academic Ant 46
People Are Suffering 46
Light 49

EPIC TALES

Excerpt From: The Scarlet Knight 52
Legend Of The Nighthorse 59
Killing The Old Nazi 70
The Whore Of Babylon 140
The Crotch Rocket 189
The Scarlet Knight Meets The Whore Of Babylon 201

THE RAPE OF ATHENA

(Written by Stevie, brother of HighPockets, to ingratiate himself with Professor Ariana, idolater and pagan, written to seduce Socherie, his daughter, a beauty beyond understanding, and written in the Greek epic style the Professor so admires, a poem published in the school media that by total happenstance then becomes integral to the recovery of a fellow student savaged by a vicious rapist-murderer, and used by her to overcome her fear and terror and come forward to confront her would-be killer in open court.)

*At any moment of time and being
the only concern of importance,
of any matter at all, is that which
makes you more alive, or less alive.
All the rest is pulp and trash.
—The Whore of Babylon*

Prologue

Sing, Nemesis, conflicted mother of her whose beauty
launched in 1000 Achaen ships those who demolished
Troy's magnificence, the glory of Priam, those who slew
Hektor, the Idol of Manhood, and caused the Niobe grief
of Andromache, those who put to wander and trek
him who set the foundations and might of sun-glorious Rome,
who then sold into slavery the children of the Achaens
who had sailed those ships and plundered Troy.

Sing, goddess, of your own retribution that even befell
down to Underworld upon the great warrior Achilleus,
and still today haunts like a dark bear sorrowed Athenians
for their wicked treachery upon Great Goddess Athena.

I

Sing, goddess, of Athena's travail, of Athena's ordeal,
she the beloved daughter of Zeus and fountainhead
of courage and wisdom, steadfast in loyalty to Zeus,
and her stalwart and true as Apollo's sun-car across
the bright blue sky, chaste and mighty as the wine dark sea,
the Sea of Poseidon, sending rains and swelling rivers
to cleanse and purify all mortals and servants of Zeus,
from Macedonia to Crete and Egypt, from Hebrides
to Persia, even to mysterious kingdoms of spice in the East.

Yes, such is Athena and mighty is she— shield, sword,
and bow on her back, riding the mountains down from Olympus
astride Valeria, the great gray horse of vanquish, as gray
as wisdom itself, with flashing hooves of solid silver,
her long black mane midnight dark, as are her forelock and socks,
and her eyes as red as her fiery nostrils, and reins of gold
from river boulders of Ranzipour— a steed created
by Zeus himself from the silver mountains of Iberia
and her heart from its amber plains, washed at her making
in waters of the Guadalquivir, where gods bathe and then
lay down beside it to rest; and given was she at once
to none but the Mighty Athena, beloved of Zeus over all
from first moment she leapt full grown and armored
from his own head cleaved by Vulcan with ax to free her,
sword and shield in hand and bow strapped to her back,
crying out defiance and roaring a shattering roar
that deafened thunder, endearing her at once and forever
to her father Zeus, Ruler of the world, the Maker of Law.

Such is Athena and mighty is she before all the world.

Yet, sing you must that from gruesome Underworld, from deepest
depth of Hell, rose Hades himself in a furious rage and anger
born of Zeus' love for Athena, and enraged was Hades
because of her endless bounty for the Achaen Raiders
against his beloved Troy, and the death of valiant Hektor
at the hands of Arrogance in flesh and the grief and tears
of Andromache, beloved wife of Hektor, and both their voices,
one from the ruins of Troy, the other by his side in Hell,
both their voices crying out for vengeance against
Athena the one who betrayed them; and Hades' rage stoked
by the loneliness of Hell as are Vulcan's fires stoked
by red molten magma plume come from deepest mantle;

and was now Hades' rage unloosed to pursue Hell's vengeance
by Zeus' lust for Leda, your daughter, whom to seduce at leisure
had he concealed himself in secrecy from Hera, his wife,
and taken form as a dark and elegant swan of delight;
and now to frolic in passion alone did Zeus gladly
abandon his throne on Olympus, and all his reign.

Thus up from Hell arose the seething Hades and snatched
from ambush the unwary Athena who had weakened herself
by slaking her thirst not with Nektor but instead a wine
created for revenge by Kronus in exile, that poisoned her zeal
and sapped her strength, a vile wine deceitfully said
to be crushed for her delight by venerable Athenians,
but handed to her by Hades, disgraced brother of Zeus,
disguised as a crook back academe in pursuit of wisdom.

Sing, goddess, how staggered Athena became in stupor
and realizing Hell's treachery upon her, called out she for help
from Zeus her father, to restore her strength in divine salvation,
but unanswered fell her pleas upon an empty throne,
and snatched was she in her weakness by raging Hades
and into the Parthenon dragged he her in her stupor,
scattering in terror all her adherents, all the priests
and priestesses who fled the face of Death and torment;
and raped he the chaste Athena beneath her statue
sculpted in massive ivory and gold by her people, and roared he
with the rage of Hell as he raped her, a roar that shook
the Parthenon like a reed in the wind, and all men fled
down the belly of their homes, shaking in fear, calling out
to the empty throne of Zeus, himself now vanished in the guise
of the Dark Swan to relish and stroke the beauty of Leda.

And so it was that Athenians without the wisdom
and presence of Athena to guide them did next day emerge
demoralized from their homes, confused and bewildered and soon
men lusted after other men's wives and daughters,
and women after other women's husbands and sons reeling,
men after men, women after women, unsatisfied,
and food consumed to sickness, and drink and drunkenness reigned,
the Academe reduced to bickering and faction and lawlessness;
and quickly were the gods and great ones forgotten and spat upon,
and Herakles remembered for merely his manly muscle,
and Bacchus only celebrated, not in righteousness
but in riotous glee, and the glory that was Achilleus'
mocked by men killing men in the streets with rocks and clubs

and women assaulted and strangled in a reeling disaster as Hades
held captive Athena in weakness and raped her daily and roared
an earth shaking roar for all to hear— and soon to cheer.

But Hera in anger with Zeus, his lust and his absence, took pity
upon the people of the golden city of Athens, a city now choking
with filth and running sewage, and foul corruption in the streets
from unburied bodies as the people sank daily more and more
into the Beast of Depravity and held up buffooning Bacchus
as the one true god and teacher, and him only worshipped,
and thrown into sewage pits were broken statues and icons
of all other gods, and cheered daily was the roar of Hades.

Injustice first, then fear and despair soon after, roamed
the streets like living Minotaurs, devouring without hesitation.

II

From Hippos, a city of trees west of Egypt, did Hera
seek and find Hestandalos the Archer, beloved husband
of Verónea, handmaiden of their queen, and loving father he
of Thea, she who would be the re-builder of the Parthenon,
and he the mortal son of Vulcan whom Hera knew
loved Athena secretly and longed to end her travail,
but powerless was he before Hades' rage, Vulcan a cripple
and without a warrior's skill or roar or battle heart;
but loved he deeply Hestandalos, his son, and child
of a woman blinded on accident by Diana hunting,
and therefore blinded was she to Vulcan's ugliness
or crippled leg and knew only caress of his hand and affection
of his voice and knew as well his godly love to match
her love for Hestandalos, who as he grew in stature learned
the skill of bow and arrow from Diana herself, in justice
for blinding his mother, justice, said Diana, learned from Athena,
and soon greater with the bow than Hestandalos only Diana.

On command from Hera an arrow was fashioned by Vulcan himself
on anvil and stone deep in his fiery cave, an arrow
tipped with blood red diamond, a rare such diamond sought
by Vulcan from deepest earth, from red molten magma,
a diamond so hard only Vulcan's right arm and unmatched skill
with hammer and stone, fire and forge, could shape a point
to sharply pierce immortal Hades, and only his neck,
and solely one spot, straight though the front of his throat
into his larynx, to silence his voice. Without voice and roar

will he then feel weakened and powerless, retreating
down to gruesome Underworld to sever the arrow and recover;
and Athena freed will guide again with wisdom and reason
the people of Athens, and will restore harmony from Hell's chaos.

Certainly Zeus soon will long for his throne, said Hera,
and return from his dalliance, and punish Hades for his horrors.
Certainly all this will happen before the death of Athens.
But still, without Zeus must Hestandolos the Archer face Hades alone.

Yet, for Hestandalos to triumph must he look Death itself
in the face and stand stalwart to launch truly the arrow
into Hades' throat. Thus only is necessity served,
and urgent soars the need because soon Athens
will corrupt itself beyond redemption— yet, empty remains
the throne of Zeus as chaos marauds the mind of man.

An agreement was soon sealed by Hera with righteous Apollo,
who loved his sister Athena and agreed he to hold
the sun-car still in the sky at far point of tomorrow,
and Hades bewildered but urgent with his rage for Athena
and deprived of the wonder and terror of night will rise up out
of the Parthenon to gawk at the deep blue sky for answer.
Only then as he gawks will his throat be exposed to arrow,
the single arrow with blood red diamond from deepest magma,
a diamond sharpened to point only by the great skill
and strength of Vulcan's right arm working tirelessly with hammer
and forge, a point to pierce the larynx and throat of Hades,
and stop at once and suddenly his roar.

"Why I," then spoke Hestandalos, "Diana is so much
better with bow. If I do this thing, when I die,
Hades will take great vengeance upon me in the Underworld.
Excruciating will be my suffering, beyond imagination."

Thus spoke Apollo and said, "I will change the course of the sun
in the sky to descend behind you on the Parthenon waiting,
and when Hades emerges to gawk, it will blind him to you,
and he will not know you, not now nor the day you cross
with Chiron the River Styx, and wash in the River Lethe
for forgetfulness.

"But why not Diana?" insisted Hestandalos. "Why not?"

Then did Vulcan rise up and speak to his beloved son:

  "No god, my son, will harm another god, only Hades
  in Hell's horror and loneliness, and only in absence of Zeus.
  He must be returned to Underworld before foundations
  of Athens crumble in corruption, and if Athens crumbles
  so goes all Greece and Africa, East and West,
  from Persia to Iberia, and in anarchy and desecration
  the entire world falls, perhaps never again to rise and flourish.

Now again spoke Apollo:

  "My grief will be intolerable then, a state of chaos,
  such that I could not manage the sun chariot across
  the sky, and all the world will plunge into darkness.
  But tomorrow will I put light in the night sky
  behind your back to blind raging Hades to you.

Said Vulcan:

  "And I will put my strength in your right arm."

Said Hera:

  "And I will make stalwart your legs to stand before him."

Said Diana:

  "And I will put my eye into your eye
  to make straight your aim, true to the throat of Hades."

Then said Hestandalos:

  "But which of you will look with me
  into mortality, into the face of Death?"

Only silence fell and Hestandalos the Archer
understood the truth— even the gods themselves fear Hades.

Still, the fear of the entire world in darkness shook
to the core his being because of his love for Verónea and Thea,
and devastated was he for Athena, violated daily
by this raging roaring godly horror, driving
all honor and wisdom from Athens, and soon perhaps the world.

"Where is Zeus?" he cried. "Tell me, where is Zeus?"

But for him there was no answer, for none but Hera
knew of Zeus' dangerous frolic with Leda and none
his day of return...like nightfall at twilight, total chaos loomed.

Thus said Vulcan to Hestandalos, "Only you
at this time and at this place, only you.
There can be no other. Of all mortals only you."

And thus spoke Hestandalos the Archer:
  "I would that I could walk away. I want
  to walk away because I know this deed
  will mean the death of me, but I cannot walk away.
  O, where is Zeus that I must do this thing and suffer?"
  I love Verónea and Thea and want to be
  with them, but where would they be in a world
  deprived of honor, wisdom, and all chastity,
  even with me to protect them and love them.
  Sooner or later will corruption consume them ruthlessly.
  Better their life without me in light than with me in darkness."

From his father's hand, from beloved Vulcan seized he
now in his hand the blood red diamond arrow.

  "Tomorrow at sundown we do this thing, if be no Zeus
  to deliver us. O, where is Zeus?"

But next day returned not Zeus, for his delight with Leda
reclined and held naked and soft in dark wings of a swan
had shown itself a peaceful delight, one unknown
since that moment Kronus disgorged his quarreling siblings;
and dallied Zeus within her affection, knowing the world
could be in chaos without him, and for these moments
while Leda totally captivated all his heart he did not care.

III

During that day the people of Athens ran amok,
those few shouting warnings of chaos themselves shouted down
and trampled by roaring mob crying out there is no god
but Bacchus and his temple needed on the Acropolis,
a temple to honor him where now stands the Parthenon;
and the mad mob drunken and thronged with lotus eaters,
careening without understanding or wisdom, rose up on a whim

to burn down the Parthenon and build bigger
a temple to Bacchus; and they set fires to Athena's temple
as sunset neared, to burn it down and Athena with it
if need be, to build the tower of raucous Bacchus
in abundant fervor and zeal for him and him only.

Hestandalos the Archer climbed the Parthenon as fires
began rising up the walls, and his back to the sun
he stood with his bow, as Apollo true to his divinity veered
the path of the sun-car and held it still in the sky.
Now Hades, aloof to mob and fire and hungry for nightfall
to loudly rape yet again the chaste Athena who lay
in stupor beneath her ivory statue, now stooped he in anger
to go out the entrance and stand tall to inspect the sun-car;
and there on the burning roof Hestandalos stood waiting,
stalwart in legs, strong in right arm drawing back
the blood red diamond arrow, his eye clear and certain
of its flight. Beneath his feet he felt the burning roof failing
and still he stood and awaited exact moment to shoot,
knowing the roof soon to collapse, and him upon it.

As Hades turned at last to gawk, a simple cloud
in blue sky blotted the sun, and stood both in shadow now,
Hestandalos and Hades. Prepared had he been and stoked
with courage to look into the face of Death while hidden
by blinding sun, but now shuddered Hestandalos in his heart,
for Death looked upon him now in his face and knew him
who would soon be dead and crossing the River Styx.

A moment is a lifetime as he fought his terror, and as the roof
creaked and sagged, he could not help himself— enthralled
deep in his being by love for Verónea and Thea
he could not flee. Without the return of Zeus to throne
he alone stood the Beast to battle. As the roof collapsed
and Hell roared, he fell into the flames knowing
that Death saw him in the shadow and now knew his face,
yet still he launched truly the blood red diamond arrow
and fell before the arrow struck, never knowing
it had struck, and struck with the force of his father's right arm,
struck and pierced did the blood red diamond arrow,
piercing directly the throat and larynx of Hades raging,
and silenced totally and at once his roar.

Away from the Parthenon staggered Hades and reeled he
backwards down the Acropolis, stumbling faster and faster,
unable to roar, and turned he and fled back, back

to the huge mouth in Acheron, north of Athens,
west of Macedonia, and down he fled, down and down
into Hell, to sever the arrow and restore his voice,
and renew his roar, and await Hestandalos the Archer,
whose face he now knew well, soon to be rowed by Chiron
over the River Styx, and into his kingdom of vengeance.

IV

As Hades, his disgorged brother fled, Poseidon heaved
a great wave up from the Aegean, up on the Acropolis,
over the Parthenon to extinguish all fires, many Athenians
drowning in the tide. Into the temple now hurried Poseidon
before 3 priests running to help their beloved Athena
and swept he into his arms an insensible ravished Athena,
blinding the 3 priests who now saw Wisdom naked.

Into his Ocean home he bore her, to cleanse and purify her,
into the wine dark sea to renew her and her goodness,
and with her goodness her honor and her wisdom, and then
did Zeus now return from his frolic with Leda, and learning
now of Hades assault upon his beloved Athena roared he
a roar that was heard from Athens to Crete, from Persia
to Iberia and the Hesperides, all the way to Africa,
past Egypt and Hippos to the source of all the crocodiles.
Even Hades in Hell heard the roar of Zeus and postponed
his vengeance upon Hestandalos the Archer, called out of Hell
as he was to the throne of Zeus on Olympus.

"Who do you think you are!" roared
Zeus to Hades

"I am who I am," cried Hades
unshaken, "and all who be
know me, and no one, not god
nor man who fears me not.
Who be you, Zeus, to abandon
your throne for a mortal woman
and thus again expose this
world to chaos."

"Give up your vengeance upon the archer,
your vengeance upon Hestandalos."

"I will not. He will suffer. What Do I have where I reside but death and loneliness and my vengeance to brood upon and make suffer those who offend me? He will suffer worse than any have ever suffered, even more than the Great Achilleus, and for all eternity."

"You do not fear my anger, Hades?"

"No. I wish no conflict ever with my beloved younger brother, the Great and Glorious Zeus Almighty, but both we know and know for certain that over these lonely eons, have I learned of Death— only of Death—and immortality, even that of Great Zeus, may not survive my piercing grasp."

"Do you think you know me so well?"

"Never for a mortal will you risk my grasp. This I know: no god will ever risk Divinity for some mortal, any mortal ever lived. No god! Especially for a dead mortal. And none return from the realm of the dead, none! For if one did, then the world collapses as we know it, and Olympus too. For a dead mortal you will not risk Divinity nor collapse of the world. This I know, as certain as I know Death itself.

Yet, as they spoke in stand-off confrontation
before all the gods on Olympus, had Athena recovered
from Hades' raging abuse and violation, and his chaos.
Filled was she now with anger, and in her endless anger
approached her Vulcan who in secret loved her,
and into her anger he came to speak for his beloved son,
Hestandalos the Archer, and of his son's courage to rescue her,
yet endless suffering now his fate, now and forever.

"Then retrieve him from Hades,"
said Great Goddess Athena.

> "I cannot. From there none
> come back and I am a cripple
> without the sword or wisdom to
> threaten Hades."

"What is that to me?"

> "He died for you."

"What is that to me, the death of a mortal,
whether today or tomorrow is only
dust in a whirling wind, surely of no
significance, and dying for a god
should fill him with gladness
crossing the River Styx."

As taught her by Poseidon, Athena whirled winds
and a typhoon around herself to separate herself
from Vulcan; but though wise and filled with understanding,
she had never known children, nor the love borne
for them, greater even than her affection for Achilleus,
the Master of Myrmidons and slayer of Hektor, first son of Priam.
Greater than affection is the love a father bears for his son,
as Priam did for Hektor.

For his son, Hestandalos the Archer,
Vulcan crossed over the typhoon fortress
into the eye of her solitude.

"Have you no compassion?" he shouted above the roar of her storm.

"I do not know what compassion is.
That is a thing for mortals, something
you saw in your son, only a mortal.
Leave me now or face suffering
equal to mine from Hades."

He pressed closer to her in her anger, the one he secretly loved.
Above the world they rose in their confrontation and all
the world could see and feel the lash of it and even
Poseidon's sea raged violently beneath them, and waves
crashed in fury and ruin on island and mainland alike.

"That which was Athena," he roared above the howl, "that which loved the people of Athens, has that been lost in this ordeal with Hades, lost and gone with him down into Hell? Has sea and Poseidon failed to restore you?"

"Be gone," she roared as loud as Hades,
"I cannot recall what I am not
nor what I can no longer be."

"Mortals can. Are they greater than gods? In your ordeal, Great Goddess, did you yourself experience mortality?"

"Be gone!"

"And that mortality has lessened you, yet mortals live it and dance and sing."

"I do not understand their joy.
A single moment of mortality
filled me with something beyond understanding,
beyond wisdom, something that almost
cracked my being. Paralyzed was I
by the touch of Hades, even more
than by the vile wine of Kronos."

"That was fear of mortality,
What mortals live with daily,
yet paralyzed are they not
within their being as was
Great Goddess Athena merely
touched by Death."

"Leave me!" howled Athena again like Hades.
"Leave me or, by Zeus, Vulcan, will I
cripple your other leg."

"Look at you," roared Vulcan to
Match Athena's howl, and
moving for love of his son
closer even than strike of her
sword. "Look at you. Look!
Great Goddess, crippled by
your own understanding. How
mighty do you consider your
own self compared to any
mortal, yet did truly my son
Hestandalos do what you could
never do, what no god, even
Zeus the Great, can ever do:
For love of his wife and child,
for love of his kind...for you did
he stand stalwart and strong,
not only in face of mortality
but also in face of eternal
wrath, a wrath you well know,
stood he tall and stalwart with
courage and saved you, Great
Goddess, saved you with blood
red diamond arrow cleanly and
bravely shot through throat of

                    Hades stopping at once upon
                    you his terror and his roar.

Immediately the typhoon ceased, and descended they back
upon the earth, face to face, goddess to god, and
the waves calmed and birds flew above the wine dark sea.

"No mortal," she said, "no mortal ever
saves a god." Gone was the wrath,
gone out of her voice, stilled now by understanding.

                    "This is true," said Vulcan.
                    "No Mortal ever saves a god."

"What now, Vulcan," said Athena, "how do
I restore myself? What can I do?
Even Poseidon and the great waters
of Ocean Sea have not truly restored me.
You are right. I am crippled as you
by my own understanding, touched for a moment
by the icy chill of mortality, and by what
I can never know as a god— in the full
face of mortality, am I as stalwart
as Hestandalos. I can never know. Does
laying down their life for a wife or child,
another, or even a god, does that make
them greater than us?"

                    "I have no answer, Great One.
                    Gods are gods and mortals
                    are not, and the greatness of
                    each is unknown to the other,
                    seen perhaps and witnessed,
                    but unknown. In your travail
                    as a god, because he is only
                    mortal, do you abandon the
                    one who delivered you? Have
                    you forgotten him who loved
                    you, and loved you well, even
                    to his death?"

A total calm had descended on 2 gods standing
face to face, near touching.

> "Restore yourself, Athena. Be
> Great again. Deliver from
> torment the one who singly
> delivered you from yours,
> even though it cost him all
> he had, or ever will have, for
> forever and ever. Be you as
> much a god to him as he was
> mortal to you, Hestandalos
> of Hippos, beloved husband
> of Verónea, father of Thea,
> son of Vulcan, archer."

Above them watched Athena the sun-car of Great Apollo
sail magnificence across the sky, pouring down warmly
upon land and waters the mystery of light and vision—
and she watched pairs of sea eagles mating fly
above the waters and over the land, and waves lapped
tenderly the shore, as a wolf her cubs, and all this did
Athena watch and gaze then see and know in her being.

Now from deep in her being like volcanic surge burst up again
what burst through her when first she sprang from the head of Zeus,
and like crack of lightning sprang now that being fully restored—
Great Goddess Athena bursting with Divinity.

On the shoulder of Vulcan lay Athena her left hand,
the only time she ever touched the one who secretly loves her.

"Vulcan has a crippled leg,
but strong his heart and stronger still
his right arm. Make for me this night,
O Vulcan, 2 blood red diamond arrows,
and I will deliver your son from torment,
or be a god no more forever."

V

Thus strapped Athena the Aegis to her armored breast,
and at sunrise upon the bare back of Valeria she leapt,
the great gray horse of vanquish, as gray as wisdom itself,

created by Zeus from Iberian mountains and her heart
from amber plains, hooves of solid silver, long black mane and
forelock, and socks as dark as midnight, eyes as fearsome red
as her fiery nostrils, and reins of gold from river boulders
of Ranzipour. Upon her she leapt and north she galloped,
north of Athens, west of Macedonia, to the Acheron
and the Temple of Hades, to the gaping mouth of the giant cave
that leads down, only down, to the Underworld of Hell.

Stopping at this terrible mouth, not knowing with certainty
her return to light, she breathed deep, a mighty breath,
and Valeria in her amber heart felt the urgency of
Great Goddess Athena, and on her hind legs rose up,
kicking dark forelegs with hooves of glistening silver,
and thus cried Athena, "On, Valeria, on my Lady,
into the mouth of Hell, my Lady," and galloped they did
into the mouth of darkness, over flinted rock
disgorged for eons from the deepest bowels of molten Hell,
and Valeria's hooves of solid silver struck that rock and sparked
spears of silver light that strobed the darkness and lit
their pathway down and down into the world of the doomed,
the world of Death, the Kingdom of Hades, eons ago
determined with Zeus and Poseidon by casting of lots.

"On, my Lady, on," she cried, down and down,
"Hades, come I now for you."

Down, down, in deepening circles, as down into
the deepest canyon, and beyond beyond beyond,
the flashing lights off silver hooves to guide them,
down they galloped, ferocity struck on Athena's face.

"On, my Lady, on my Lady," and the sound echoing in the caverns
of 1000 hooves and her voice a horde of Myrmidons shouting,
the sparkling lights of flinted silver eerie as a ghostly army.
"On, my Lady. On my Lady. Hades, come I now for you."

Down and down they rode in swaddling timelessness,
then over the River Styx in a leap so mighty that Charon
fell in fright on the black waters, and soaring over Lethe
in equal godly might, she knocked Cerberus senseless
with shield at the Gates of Hell itself, roaring and crashing
through the gates that ripped like thornbush Africanus,
past faceless souls that cringed in horror, and countless others
calling out to her from despair and hopelessness.

"On, my Lady, on," she cried, down and down,
past heroes and bad men crowding the way to the throne room
of Hades; and rising on hind legs burst Valeria with silver hooves
through doors of serpents entwined, and into a throne room foul
they galloped and stood in silvery presence, horse and rider,
that stunned and shocked all there present, even himself,
the insufferable Hades, who stood and roared his rage
at the silver sight of the echoing thundering Athena on Valeria.

"So your voice is restored," she roared,
an equal to Hades. "So is my strength
and here I take no wine from you.
In one hand my sword and the other my shield
and standing in quiver 2 blood red diamonds,
their heads forged by the hand of Vulcan.
With blood red diamonds I take your eyes;
and with sword take that with which you violated me;
your voice I leave unscathed in the dark
to roar your pain for all eternity.

"What do you want, Daughter
of Zeus? Be wary lest you be
touched again by mortality."

"You yourself take heed, Beast.
Someone now of full body and strength,
someone once again formidable,
with understanding of the art of battle,
someone with sword and wisdom can turn
back upon yourself your severed hand
and someone can on you inflict
that with which you threaten me."

"What do you want, Great
Goddess?"

"I want back my chastity."

"How can you take back that
being—a being I took and
discarded?"

"You never took it!" Athena roared
in a thunder that sent all souls in
the throne room to their knees, even Hektor.
"You tried to steal it but it cannot be stolen.
It must be given and I did not give it,
not then, not now, not ever. But lose it
I do each day I abandon to you the one
who loved me and served me and gave me his life
and for his people as well. Give me the archer.
Give me Hestandalos, son of Vulcan.

> "No, I will not. You think you
> can restore his life?"

"Give me Hestandalos!"

> "Are you willing to risk
> mortality to take him?"

"And you, are you willing to risk
mortality to keep him?"

Now from the bare back of Valeria leapt Athena
and rushed the throne of Hades, and with shield and Aegis
knocked him from it and over him stood, sword in hand,
and Hades saw her willing to risk Divinity for this mortal,
but not he, and he knew fear for the first time ever,
and his strength drained.

> "I give him to you," he quickly
> conceded. "Can you restore his
> life and love?"

"No, but I can end his torment."

"But what of me, goddess? What of Hades? What do I have exiled here to this Underworld, to this Hell? The Great Goddess Athena proudly roams the world astride a magnificent steed. What of me? Eternal separation is all I know, managing the dead, an endless isolation by cast of lots. For brief time assaulting you did I stall my alienation and loneliness. Who will end my torment?"

"What is that to me, Beast?" cried Athena. "I relish your torment. Give me Hestandalos the Archer, or face battle."

"Find him yourself if save him you must. As for godly battle, perhaps the torment of mortals and the Sea of Oblivion dwarf the torment of Hades."

Then she heard a piercing scream that rattled all of Hell,
the scream of pain and despair of Hestandalos the Archer;
and bursting through basaltic walls she found him
in his ordeal, chained to a pendulum, swinging slowly
through a molten magma white hot as the sun itself
that forms deep in the earth blood red diamonds of fire.
In excruciating agony suffered Hestandalos his torments,
maintained in flesh by Hades to magnify his pain.

In his eyes when he saw her arose a vision of magnificence
Athena had never seen, beyond love and gratitude,
and in her wisdom was it now she understood—
there in his eyes seeing her crashing through to deliver
him from Hades, there in his eyes shone a mortal's hope
as deep and blue as the rippling sea, and burst salvation
as clear and true as sunlight itself, bursting there in his eyes
in this the darkest pit of Hell, and moved was the Goddess Athena,
moved by his eyes was she, eyes brimming with hope and salvation,
the son of Vulcan, Hestandalos the Archer.

With her sword she severed the pendulum and its crystal chains.
Upon her back she swung him and upon Valeria she leapt,
his arms around her forehead, his legs beneath her breasts.

"Hold on to me," she cried. "Do not
let go, for by Zeus is it vowed,
I will ride you out of Hell
or be a god no more forever."

Out of the throne room they trotted to gallop,
but there stood Hades blocking their path, pushing someone
towards them, and startled was she by the eyes of Achilleus.

"Help me, O Athena," pleaded Achilleus.
"Do not abandon me to torment."

"Which one, Great Goddess,"
cried Hades now, "Can you save
them both? Which one, or be by
vow immortal no more."

In silvery presence she rode in circle around the two.
On her back she could feel the pain of Hestandalos
and see in dark eyes the despair of Achilleus, mighty Achilleus,
Master of the Myrmidons, slayer of Hektor in bloody vengeance
at the walls of Troy, in sight of wailing Andromache.
Deep into her wisdom she searched as she circled,
and Hades smug with vengeance stood to block their passage,
and the great Achilleus now reduced to a beggar of mercy.

"I cannot change the fate of mortals
nor change the scheme of mortality.
Only can do that one greater than I,
greater even than the mighty Zeus.
But this one in torment who died for me,
saving him I restore myself."

She continued the two to circle in her silvery presence,
goddess and steed, exploring the depth of her wisdom.

"Hades," she said, "a mortal woman you love,
Persephone, Demeter's daughter."

                              "How do you know this?"

"I will not oppose you with Demeter
to make Persephone queen and to honor her,
in your way. But in return for me,
now and forever, you take no vengeance
on any mortal who has ever loved me,
now and forever. Make your choice—
vengeance on mine or end of torment,
the end of loneliness forever with Persephone."

At once Hades released Achilleus, who turned faceless
and shrunk back into the sea of faceless souls unending.

"You honor her and honor mine,
or return I will and one of us
will soon be mortal, and face forever
this Sea of Oblivion."

Hades stepped aside and blocked no more the goddess,
and threatened no more the ones who loved her.

"I am Athena," she cried. "I am again formidable."

She reached her arm around to hold the back of Hestandalos,
and Valeria felt her urgency and reared up on hind legs again.

"Hold tight, Hestandalos," Athena shouted.
"We will deliver you this day.
Go, my Lady. Take heart, my Lady.
Ride us out of Hell, my Lady."

Into a gallop they bolted, up towards the mouth of Hell,
stopping only at the River Lethe to drink and restore
his memory, that of his wife and daughter, and again
to bathe him in the River Styx and cease his pain
and to stand on the bank again the drenched ferryman Chiron.

Up, up the circles of Hell Valeria galloped,
Hestandalos' arms tightly around Athena's forehead
and tightly his legs beneath her breasts, and strobing from hooves
sparks of silver light that flashed again his memories of
wife and child among the sounds of 1000 horses
and the shouts of a horde of Myrmidons, "On, my Lady,
on my Lady. Up, up the circles of Hell, my Lady,"
the mighty Valeria faltering never, up, up,
to the mouth of Hell they galloped and stood as Athena had promised,
Hestandalos safely delivered from Hell's vengeance and torment.

In her quiver as they rode had he seen the blood red diamond arrows
and now he held them to feel the love and strength of his father.

"To magnify your torment," she said, "has Hades maintained
your body, but I cannot restore you to your life,
that would alter Olympus, and the earth itself,
and needs one greater than I, and even Zeus."

> "Yes, I understand," he said.
> "Yet grateful am I for my
> memory restored and
> grateful more forever for
> my deliverance."

She watched him fondle the blood red diamond arrows of his father,
turning them slowly in his hands, remembering those he had died for,
and the Great Goddess Athena too, and she knew it.

"But can I yes do something else,
yet to your eternal liking. Yes."

Sing, Nemesis,
how away to his home she bore him, to Hippos, the city of trees,
and in their courtyard in the night, as his wife and daughter
slept in aching sorrow, she turned him upside down
with his father's blood red diamond arrows in his hands.

"Be formidable forever," he cried, "Great Goddess Athena."

Upside down in the courtyard buried she him, his fingers
and arms to his delight now become roots, his head now bole,
his shoulder and waist then turned to trunk, his stalwart legs

become limbs stretching for sunlight and warmth, and all
his flesh once maintained in Hell for endless torment
now become by Athena's being blossom, flower, and leaf.
The blood red diamonds like sap rose up through him, through root
and bole and trunk and limbs, filling the flowers to brim
in blood red color, a color that marvels the eye of all
who behold it, red mimosa, a tree of rare beauty.

At dawn mother and child found to their delight
the red mimosa tree, and wife found in swinging on limbs
and daughter on climbing of branches that all grief
seeped away and they only remembered and felt the love of
husband and father as he gathered them within his embrace,
and in his happiness spewed he seed that spread red mimosa
throughout the world and in every tree he felt himself
and though he could not hear nor see he felt his being
scattered through all red mimosa, wherever they grew,
and in due time he embraced the children of his daughter
and her children's children, and by the grace of Athena
and her wisdom would he know the touch of all his descendants,
and to this day, each day, in sunshine or cool of twilight
he feels swinging in his welcoming limbs and climbing his red-budded
branches the laughter and joy of the children of all his descendants,
and to show them his love and remembrance spreads he freely
beneath him upon the earth seed and leaf in abundance.

Such was the bounty of Athena to Hestandalos the Archer
who with his life freed her from torment of Hades
and taught her being of hope and salvation beyond understanding.

Sing, goddess, of Athena's forgiveness then for the people of Athens,
their debauchery and their treachery, and of her return
to guide them, and in coming years of the Parthenon restored
by the aegis of Thea, daughter of Hestandalos the Archer,
to whom as she grew gave Athena the knowledge of building
and the wisdom to know both where and how to build with strength.

Yet, sing, goddess, that though forgiveness flowed for repentance,
still, with forgiveness comes also painful consequence:
in the wars with Sparta, though called upon in daily prayer
by the people of Athens, she would not intervene, not once,
not then nor in any war since that time of chaos.
The city since has suffered great outrage and torment,
and she took no pleasure in any of it, only justice.

Sing also, goddess, of the times she crosses path of Vulcan,
who bows always in gratitude and in his heart
holds secret his love for Great Athena.

Sing, Nemesis, of Great Goddess Athena, chaste Athena,
who leapt defiant from the cloven head of mighty Zeus,
and through the eons and generations of winding time
has known the male touch of two, only two—
the violent assault and treachery of the immortal Hades
and the grateful embrace of the mortal Hestandalos of Hippos,
arms around her forehead and legs beneath her breasts;
and whose eyes wide with hope and salvation, like sea and sunlight,
astonished the wise and understanding Athena, of all the gods
of Olympus the only one through all the eons and eons of time
who freely chose to risk Divinity for a mortal.

Rationalist Lament

(Poem written by Stevie for his college magazine)

What magic is this that I deny
that ripples the pool behind my eye
then swirls and shudders on down my spine.

"Comes not from God, 'tis not divine,"
with thousands I cry. "Bourgeoise heresy!
Good Christians are we, Black Sorcery,
and burn we the sinners that practice thee."

Such fools we are. What hypocrisy!
When magic is brewed and spells are cast,
where stands the man worships not the Black Mass?

To Be or Not To Be

*(Poem originally written by Stevie in high school,
immersed in the depths of depression,
now published in the SF State Herald))*

Once in a newspaper I read
of a man who felt we are better dead,
and this to paper having said,
he put a bullet though his head.

Tell me now, man better dead,
is it true what I read,
what your last handwriting said?
Should *we* put bullets through our heads?

Poor Man's Dilemna

Though I spoke with cogent logic
and though I spoke with cogent voice,
   I lacked essential authority—
I had a Honda, he a Rolls-Royce

God Bless Ben Franklin

What a miracle are spectacles!
Tactile am I without…
World wide with.

Sound of Hope

(Another Stevie depression poem)

Blacked-back seagull, huge, sailing over calm sea, 2 days empty, hungry chics on rocky shore waiting. Sun setting, weather plunging, **thick fog gathering**…
Look below…flopping tuna, bleeding…**sharks**! Dive, risky, splash, grab…
Full beak now…**Jaws!, Jaws! Rise! Rise!**.. Turn home quickly. **Fly! Fly!**
All fog…total fog…**Blind fog blind**…Instincts failing… Lost pattern…
Last chance with food… Full flapping blind…**Burst out rising!**
Cliffs in sight!…**Coming home**…heart beating…
Cloaca contracts, single turd ejected.
Silent fall…striking
the water…
ploop.

Gaining Consciousness
(To learn is to venture—Vercingetorix)

Alone in a Century Graveyard

Many dreams once… many tears.
   Who remembers?
Long grass lapping on silent stones…

Comes Regret

Profound it drops me to my knees:
   exhaust from life dynamic…
Rise up and thrive! Rise up!
Without regret means void of venture
   and absolutely maker of nothing.

Comes Consciousness

Shrouded in darkness I now awake…
   strength surges…shell cracks…
Morning sun upon my face.

Warrior
**Strength of a young Greek
Beside a spirited steed,
Rippling shoulders, gentle hands.**

Singing Blues with My Father
(With a nod to Carl Sandburg)

[A Torch Poem written by Stevie when he learned secret talks were underway by SF State to bring special schooling for the mentally retarded as part of their humanities outreach, a poem that mysteriously caught the heart of the campus)

['Pruno' is an alcoholic drink convicts make in secret.]

Yes, my father is retarded
   and I am not.
Still he loves me
   with all his heart.
Of this I have no doubt.

Yes, my mother too was retarded
   and now she's dead,
killed by a drunk driver last year
   while crossing the street,
   careful to stay in the crosswalk
   and go only when the little man turned green,
and she died anyway,
   doing exactly what she had been taught.

No. I don't blame anyone for that,
   except the drunk of course,
     who is now doing a dime
     for manslaughter at Soledad,
       making pruno now his only ambition.

Yes, I miss the loving hand of my mother,
   even though I am nearly 21.
     This I do not tell anyone,
   especially not my father,
     who misses her mysteriously
     in a way he can never fathom.

Yes, if I told my father my pain,
   he would feel awful for me,
      a burden he does not understand nor need,
   and I am happy to bear it alone—
      I guess that's growing up.

Yes, my father will sometimes spend
   all day mowing "the green grass,"
      a lawn you or I could mow in 30 minutes,
         45 max.
   Stumbling by drunks on the street
      sometimes wave friendly at him,
   and he waves back, friendly,
         never making connection between them
            and my mother's slayer.

Yes, it pleases him to walk behind the power motor,
   his Center of the Universe, all day if necessary
   to make neat "the green grass,"
      sometimes running the same line multiple times,
      sometimes stopping the mower to pursue discovery.

Yes, a week ago I found the mower still warm
   and my father lying inside
   the huge cardboard box the new sofa came in,
      the sofa my mother had wanted and ordered,
   what my father and me now call Sophia the Sofa for laughs.

Loudly from inside Sofia's box
   he answered that he was finding out
      if the dark during the day is the same
      as the dark during the night,
         so I crawled in with him
            in cramped space.

      "And what are you <u>learning</u>, Dad?"

                    "That dark is dark at any time,
                    and light is light."

      "And what will you <u>do</u> with that?"

"Well I'm <u>not</u> going to live in a box,
That's for sure...I really miss your
Mother, Jeddy."

"I do too, Dad."

"I'd live in a box if that would bring
her back. That's for sure."

"If you lived in a box, Dad,
she wouldn't <u>wanna</u> come back."

*(My dad laughed.
He thought that so funny.)*

"No way, would she, that's for sure.
Let's go out and finish mowing
the green grass."

"I'll save the box, Dad. We can always
go back in it later," I said, and dragged
the huge thing beside the garage.

Yes, for an hour or so in the house
I lay on Sophia and remembered my mom
and how easy it was to make her laugh,
and remembered her angrily saying,
"I'm his mom. I can raise him without your help,"
and then her whispering in my ear,
"Let these do-gooders eat their hearts out, Jeddy.
You're such a good boy you make it easy."

And being a good boy for my mom
a<u>lways</u> my first ambition.

When again I went back outside,
my dad, though not yet finished mowing,
was sitting on a planter my mom and he
had made with concrete bricks,
the sofa box now all torn up
and piled neatly by the garbage can.

"Didn't you want to save that box, Dad?"

"No, that won't bring your mom back."

"Nothing, Dad, will bring her back."

"No, it won't. Why do we have such pain, Jeddy?"

"I don't know, Dad."

"Your mom would not want me to have such pain."

"No, she wouldn't."

"Then why did she die like that?"

"She didn't want to."

"Of course she didn't want to. You Don't know any more than me, and you go to college and read books."

(My father is awed by big books and those who read them.)

"Some questions have no answers, Dad, not even in books."

"Well, that's a disappointment."

"Maybe you already know the answer, Dad."

"Love is pain, Jeddy."

"Sooner or later, Dad."

"If I had not loved your mom, I would not have this pain."

"That's true, Dad."

"But then I wouldn't have you either.

"Well, that's true too."

"I can take the pain."

"You're my hero, Dad."

"You mean like Batman?"

"No, I mean like you, Dad.
Batman would give his mask
to be my Dad."

"You think so?"

"I know so. <u>That</u> I learned
in books."

"Well, if books say so, then that's for
sure. It's good to be your hero,
Jeddy. Now I'll finish mowing all
the green grass."

My dad was cheerful again,
as I always remembered him being.
After all these years
I was happy to do

something for him
who all my life
had given me nothing but love,
unconditional love,
the only kind he knows how.
You eat your hearts out,
you do-good mother <u>fuck</u>ers,
Yes!

Oberón's Variati on a Theme by Dylan

(Written in her study as Stevie and Mary Madelin practiced over and over but failed to master to satisfaction Dylan's song, 'Shelter from the Storm')

It was for me another life
that pitched me up here from the flood.
Blackness seemed my only hope,
the road was full of blood.
I struggled through the desert heat,
a creature void of form.
"Come in," you said, "I'll give you
shelter from the storm."

I was burned out and exhausted,
pillaged of all my truth,
poisoned down between my thighs
by chaos from my youth,
haunted by my sinfulness,
worthy of only scorn.
"Come in," you said, "I'll give you
shelter from the storm."

Beautiful Esmeralda
was whom you thought me there,
and put your smile upon my lips
and flowers in my hair.
You came to me courageously
and snatched my crown of thorns.
"Come in," you said, "I'll give you
shelter from the storm."

Today you're here in Anda-lus,
but soon must cross the line,
and beauty walks a razor's edge—
some day it won't be mine.
If I could only stop the clock
while one is only one.
"Come in," you said, and I took it,
shelter from the storm.

There are many different instruments in the symphony.
Silly to pick only one and call it the truth.

—Oberón Baranskya

[*For Hijito, mi caballero y coracón*]

For Oberón:
Another variation on a Theme by Dylan
(Sarah)

*(Composed by Stevie just before his
final departure from Málaga)*

I lay on the sand and embraced the day
when I arrived here in Málaga and came to the beach.
You lay down beside me, a whisper away.
You were coming so close, and so within reach.

*Obero-o-ón...O, Oberón...
so much happened to change your mind.
Oberón...Oberón...
so easy to look at, so hard to define.*

You lay in the sand, you were amber and sleek,
and reached out to touch me in the morning sunrise.
By the cool of the evening your hand on my cheek,
your shoulders were naked, there was love in your eyes.

*Obero-o-ón...O, Oberón...
Eternal angel, sweet bird of my youth.
Oberón...Oberón...
Radiant jewel, mystical truth.*

How did I meet you, I just don't know,
a friend she brought me to protect you from harm.
I was there when you needed, there for your kiss,
there in your heart in the violent storm.

*Obero-o-ón...O, Oberón...
It's all so clear I can now understand.
Oberón...Oberón...
Loving you is the one thing that makes me a man.*

Riding wild horse over mountain and stream,
East of Eden with a daughter of Cain.

You calling down God on a friend in my arms,
bathing our sins in a shower of rain.

Obero-o-ón...O, Oberón...
Dark Lady Moor in a red Spanish lace.
Oberón...Oberón...
You must forgive me my unworthiness.

Now the beach is deserted, except for some kelp,
and a mast of a sailboat that lies on the shore.
I'll always respond should you need my help.
Just give me a map and a key to your door.

Obero-o-ón...Oberón...
Ancient queen with a radiant glow.
Oberón...Oberón...
I don't want to leave you, I don't want to go.

Miss Mary Madelin's Creed

**(Born on the same day at the same hospital, Stevie and Mary,
knowing and relying on each other since they first could crawl,
as close as twins all their lives, brother and sister.)**

Remember:

The here and now is where we live;
The past is what we learn from,

>and success can truly be measured
>by the pain endured to achieve it.

Your life, your success is limited only
by how much pain you will tolerate today
   before you quit.

What do you get, you ask,
   when you persevere through pain
     and reach success?

More pain…if you're lucky.

So buckle up, Asshole—
   let's roll!

Healer's Dilemna

**Migraine woman…
Scarlet Pax Roman shadows.
— Overwhelmed are my hands.**

Hot Summer Day

**Summer breezes so welcome on my cheek….
and youick,
Mizzer Mozquizos**

Come into Me

(Beautiful Lady　　　　　　　　　　**by**　　　　　　　　　　(La Belle Dame
with scarlet gratitude)　　　　　　　　　　　　　　　　　　avec merci rouge)

Anette Lelie

*(Written by Anette after her rescue by Stevie from kidnap
and murder, Anette broken hearted because her rejection
of him totally out of misconception and misunderstanding,
and now she realizes the truth of his heart and hers.)*

I

Come into me, my beautiful man,
   come into me my dark-eyed knight,
no need to be my strength tonight,
   come into me and let me love you.

Let tonight me be your scarlet Dame.
   Let tonight me be your red, red rose,
   and tonight me be your naked lady,
and naked show you my scarlet love.

No need to be on watch tonight,
   alert to me and keenly brood.
No need villainy to brave,
   nor staunchly guard against the flood.

II

Come into me and let me love you,
   the one you taught be unafraid.
Let me be your grateful Lady,
   and naked show you a woman's love.

Let my arms and flesh surround you
   let the scent of me be your delight.
   Let my fire and heart come warm you,
and fearless love complete the night

Come into me my beautiful man,
   come into me my dark-eyed one
   and naked me be your red, red rose
whose heart your heart has braved and won.

Malagueña Faerie Queen

*(Written by Stevie after his return to college from Málaga,
his last poem published before enlisting in the Marines.)*

A malagueña knew I once in a foreign land,
   touched my heart and deepened it mysteriously.
Young and shallow-watered was I then
   like the scarlet and stunning bougainvillea

on your garden wall, eyeful of delight, you said,
   but innately willing to dominate
     all color below.

By chance from a portico I saw you bathe,
   your nakedness stopped my breath in moan.
Not naked like a maiden, no, nor shyly sweet and lithe,
   but brazen and comfortable as a woman known.

Such stunning beauty in the evening shade,
   not the rose, dark malagueña, but the vine
     from which all roses grow.

Into your heart I poured my moral mumble—
   from your beauty I will not turn my eyes away,
how it pitched my mind into rumble and stumble,
   but my body to dreams of dance and sway.

And that same night into my eager arms you lay
   and being a Faerie Queen you raised me up
     to manly show.

Such magical voyage in life, so sweet and beguiling,
   but like gestation timed, and soon one just must be born,
no matter how difficult and tearing the de-conciling.
   You loved me but struggled with me to be gone.

Truth is, the farewell of a Faerie Queen cannot be stayed.
   Home, weathered am I now, deep watered by a spirit
     no more will I know.

Widow's Take on Tennessee Williams

*(Widow is the code name of Stevie's sniper comrade,
and is the name Stevie always uses talking of him.)*

How calmly does the golden branch
observe the sky begin to blanch,
without a cry, without a prayer,
with no betrayal of despair.

Then shortly comes the broken stem,
the plummeting to earth and then
an intercourse not well designed
for beings of a golden kind.

How calmly does that olive branch
observe the sky begin to blanch,
without a cry, without a prayer,
with no betrayal of despair.

O, Courage, could you not as well
select a second place to dwell,
not only in that golden tree,
but in the frightened heart of me.

Portrait of Jennie, a Movie, 1953

**Then with my mom: in darkness I sob.
On T.V. now: alone,
I weep for her.**

Be Thou Still in the Moonlight

(Stevie's answer to Anette's
La Belle Dame avec Merci Rouge)

Be thou still in the moonlight, your grace,
   and let a man behold you.
Be thou still in the moonlight, my lady,
   so moist and fresh from misting shoals,
and the warm breeze around you swirling
   sweet radiant summer scent.
Be thou still in the moonlight, your grace,
   and astonish a lonely soul.

Like a fire that childishly hugs you,
   your hair down nape and shoulder rolls.
Like polished jade your eyes are gleaming
   under domes of burnished brows.
Like beacons of light your face and smile
   stir and thrill a heart gone cold.
Be thou still in the moonlight, your grace,
   and let a man behold you.

How the moonlight washes your blush
   like waters have washed your radiant flesh.
Soft round boats with cranberry lamps,
   your breasts peer through your flaming tress.
Proud shoulders and a woman's courage
   lift those beamish breasts of youth.
With open arms and open hands
   you call me to sweet Xanadu.

What long smooth legs and hearty slopes
   point me to your fiery strand,
where intoxicating is scent of the rose
   and sweet its dew for an unworthy man.
Be thou still in the moonlight, your grace,
   and let me a man behold you.
Be thou still in the moonlight
   and let the world come still around you.

Chapultapec (Los Niňos Heroes)

**Fierce warriors at our walls,
soon blood, soon terror…
How juicy sweet this mango.**

A Nod to Pogo and Mahatma

Of all the demons and devils that have trod this earth,
of all the monsters that have plagued us,
the worst is the teacher defines our worth
as mind or pride or parades of lust.

Of all the gangsters and killings our streets endure,
of all the lying leaders and felonious monks,
some special hell should be reserved
for polluted judges and media skunks.

Of all the plagues of wars and pestilence,
of all the madmen spewing malevolence,
surely the worst is the savage violence
from fear of age or death—or Benevolence.

If we have seen the enemy and they is us,
if this be our tragedy from the very start,
then the battle for life on the Cosmic Bus
is Good-and-Evil raging in every heart.

QUOTE
(Overheard in Starbucks While Alone With My Notebook)

When it comes to time and life:
  it's like taking a ship home after staying in another country.
  It really doesn't matter much what you do aboard it.
  It only matters *how* you do it. It's all shuffleboard.

How's that?

It's all about having fun.
  Say you win the Ship Shuffleboard Championship on the ship home,
  and you do it by intimidation or deceit or cheating or whatever.
    What do you take home with you?
  Now suppose you come in close 2nd or 3rd or even last,
  and you have fun and everyone around you has fun.

Shuffleboard?

Yes. Which one do you prefer, winning or having fun.?

What does fun mean?

Now that's what life is all about, isn't it?

I don't get it. Maybe winning is that guy's only way to have fun.

I can't tell you how to have fun, but I can tell you what happens when you're having it.

What's that?

There's life where there wasn't any, and more life where it already is.

That's what fun is?

You betcha.

How do you know for sure?

People are laughing.

Penitent Man
by
Monsignor Christopher Walsh

(The Monsignor is Stevie's childhood mentor)

All alone in the world is a penitent man,
struggling in sorrow, in torment of prodigal self.
From where comes peace? From where can forgiveness flow?
New life, new flesh, self-hate released in pan-
oramic gesturing?... No... Before him twelve
penances rise in gauntlet: Pain bestows
no glory. Heartache achieves no honor; nor rending.
Bargaining is fruitless, like praying to redwoods.
Promises are easy and resolutions grate.
Ransom is a mild success, but defending
pointless. Coyness and shame are sycophantic falsehoods.
From surrender, only surrender, flows freedom from Fate.
    With surrender comes vision of what must be done.
    Take all that is I, O Lord—restore The One.

I Would Love You Better Now

Mocha Woman, sidling by me,
speaks love, eyes of fear,
—Inn for a pilgrim.

Sunrise Prayer
by
Monsignor Christopher Walsh

(One of Stevie's mentors
and translator from Latin of the saga
Taranis the Helvetian)

Out of the depths of righteousness,
out of the spring of hope,
comes yet another kindly spirit
to tether me to Divinity.

How many times, O lord, in weakness
fail I myself and thee?
How many times, O Lord, blinded,
call I to thee in fear?

How many times, O Lord,
besot by Good and Evil,
staggering in the mystery of Light,
reach I out to Love?

Always cry I unworthy: Thou art God to me.
Always from depths a spirit: to bind me free.

Smooch, the Fat Feline, Neglected

Ancient queen distraught,
Food scattered on a sill,
—Too tall for <u>you</u> to leap.

Academic Ant

Tragedy, horror, self-loathing...
Pain, chaos...
—Artiste on the job

People Are Suffering

Always:

They come from around the world to tug your heart
and maneuver it like a Spanish Galleon into their Tortuga...
and there commences the stripping, the fleecing, and all of it
to fill their coffers...
— all for some good cause, of course
— After all, people are suffering.

Always:

They have pictures and posters of calamity and the sobs
and images of little children amid the horrors of life...
— so unfair, so unfair,
— a little of your Great Wealth can feed them and heal them
and save them all.... Or so they plead, the jowly ones,
the talking heads, from a limousine, with a charity account
and a chauffer named Al Truism.,
— After all, people are suffering.

Always:

For fame they cry and beat their breast, and when their genuine
tears move you, they shake the cup and call for you to join them
with Great Heart and deep Sensitivity, yes, to be one of them,
to save actors from time and fire dancers from fire (Don't look
at the camera, please).
 — After all, people are suffering.

Always:

They point a finger of shame and call you a sinner or glutton or pig
or "ist"-hole or some sort of 'hole, and demand you rise to their level
of consciousness and pay your fair share to cool the deserts and liberate
the homicidal and bell the man-eaters… you first of course…
 — After all, people are suffering.

Always:

They point to a Stalin type and laud him with stunning accolades
and tearful eloquence, and honor his bloody courage, the Lord High
Protector, a unite-er, an enemy slayer, and they proffer the waves of
booty and abundance that will flow from his bounty to us, should we
choose him:

 — surely he is a river to his people…
 — And after all, people are suffering.

Always:

They are the solution, yes. They will prevail. It's God's will, or White
Man's Burden, or Manifest Destiny, a chicken in every pot, the Hun's
a coming, the only good Injun, New Deal, 54-40 or fight, remember the
Maine, all marriage is rape, the Yellow Peril, Affirmative Action now,
win one for the Gipper, it's only fair, it takes a village, oh yes, the Silent
Majority, Cultural Revolution, Tippeecanoe and Tyler too, and (for me
my personal favorite), "I like Ike."
 — they see but will not accept
 — they feel and cannot forgive

    — they storm the Bastille
        (as long as they have tenure
        and the guns are silent
        or at least the bullets blank)
            — And after all, people are suffering.

Revelation!!
Big Flash!!
This just in:
    We all suffer the same amount— 100 percent!
    No one suffers more than any one else.

  So,
    love one another or die.
    Bind up each others' wounds, or not.
    No body suffers anymore than anybody else.
    Anyone tells you different is a scoundrel
      reaching through your heart
      to rifle your wallet…

Always!

LIGHT

Definition

Photon: The smallest possible packet of light, smaller by far than any atom. If our solar system were an atom, then a photon would be the full moon lighting up the night sky.

Fact

To illuminate our lives, a photon of light once created in our star by massive violent collision of hydrogen atoms, this photon will circulate the sun's depths perhaps a million years or more before per chance it breaks out, then warps nine minutes across space to this tiny earth, glancing and dancing, and then flashes into our eye to light the moment before vanishing forever and ever, (the eye itself formed and empowered by aeons and aeons of evolution).

Remember then, my friend, every time you see in the sunlight someone you love frolicking and delighting you, that sunlight is nearly 20 times older, count it, 20 times older than human being itself, not just back to cavemen but 20 times older than that, all that light around you today, 20 times older than Neanderthals, that sunlight upon you every day and all the moonlight at night, and even older are the eyes you see it with.

Perhaps, if we be wise, we would restrict our vision to the pursuit of beauty, only beauty, and leave all sorrows and suffering and especially all evil to other less delicate organs to contemplate.

VISION

All amber and cream
   on a lonely beach,
naked arises my love
   from the sea at sunset.

Behind her the orange wafer star
   stands massively a moment on the gentle sea
     and throws a scarlet sky behind her—
   stands a golden moment before my eyes
     and frames her rising and shedding sea.

She sees not and feels not the soft light upon her
    traveled such millions of miles and years,
nor sees nor feels the carpet of sparkle
    that lays down behind her from benevolent sun
        and spans in an instant the endless sea,
    laying down upon her an amber cape
        in a moment of shimmering glistening gold,
            spectacularly,
enthusing my eyes
and startling my soul.

From the hissing sibilant sea she arises,
   a mystery to me in the playful foam,
salty ripples lapping her legs,
   like puppies an arriving mistress.

She swings her head
   to free her sopping braids
      and two fall wet,
         sliding down her breasts,
            buttery straps
               on a tawny gown.

Before her,
   only her shadow she sees,
      moving faintly on the amber sand,
   and again she swings the sopping braids,
      lifting towards me her eyes,
         —A Vision—

She sees the surprise of me
   holding wide her orange towel,
a swimming seal stitched in scarlet
    all along its total length,
    as scarlet as the brilliant sky behind her.

A broad smile bursts upon her face,
   adding its light to the glistening gold.

Unembarrassed, unashamed, and unaware
   of her naked body awash
      in this infinite moment of cosmic radiance,

she hurries to me
    and pirouettes within that scarlet seal,
    laughing delightedly within her chill.

My heart is stopped
    as she stops
        face to face
            gleaming jade eyes,
full frontal woman
    through aeons evolved
red aglow this moment
    with silkie sleek concupiscence.

Her arms surround me
    like the warm sea behind her,
        peaceful...certain...eternal...

I am enthralled.

II

Great God,
what have I possibly done
to merit such a gift,
such life and love?
What dragon slain,
what child saved,
what thought from chaos snatched,
what deed done
to deserve her worldly love
and affection dear?

Would I knew
I would do it again,
Great God,
and whatever bountiful gift bestowed,
I would on bended knee give it her
so that whatever her life
wherever her journey
she should always know
her own worth
and the wonder of my love.

EPIC TALES

Excerpt from:
The Scarlet Knight
Book I
Part I

The Death of the Ball Turret Gunner

From my mother's sleep I fell into the State,
and I hunched in its belly till my wet fur froze.
Six miles from earth, loosed from its dream of life,
I woke to black flak and nightmare fighters.
When I died they washed me out with a hose.

—Randall Jarrell 1914-1965

If I were an Indian, you'd call me Stevie Two-Fathers,
   for if anybody ever had two fathers, it was me—
      my own father and his brother—
      my beloved Uncle Tom, The Scarlet Knight;
         and he surely is the bravest man who ever lived
      about whom nobody knows a goddamn thing.

O, his family does, some, and his comrades too, a few of them,
   but even they don't know the whole of it,
not even Aunt Charlotte, them now married near 40 years.

Just me, only me…I know the whole of it,
   not every detail perhaps, The Tale of the Scarlet Knight,
but the whole of it I know.
Just me…only me.

He is a hero nobody knows who the hell he is,
    never a word about him in book or press until me now,
because Uncle Tom is a mega child killer…mega…
    since he was 24 years old,
and lived all his life in that horror and agony—
    abandoned by the military and most comrades as well,
cast into the virtual dungeon where secreted are those Americans
who commit mega atrocities and crimes against humanity,
    but yet can be covered up and never come to trial,
        America avoiding the shame of it
        and the indelible stain of it,
            and the burden upon the military
            for God only knows how long—
        all avoided,
a child killer…nothing lower than that…a child killer…
    the absolute worst humanity has to offer.

Thus Uncle Tom's name was placed on a secret list,
    a list of successfully covered up American atrocities,
    a list designed to be set aside and later mislaid,
        if not forcibly forgotten,
and Uncle Tom himself thought that the best thing to do.

But the pain his deeds caused him, what he endured for his country,
    physically, mentally, and spiritually… especially spiritually,
        a child killer, the burden of that on his soul,
        every day of his entire adult life,
that pain just should never be forgotten,
    a man who to me is my hero of heroes.

Nicht keine, Uncle Tom. Nicht keine.

First Things First

Also what must now be addressed is the embarrassment of his name,
    for whenever I speak of him, Uncle Tom,
    a racial sensibility sets in that he himself never had,
        never an untoward look on his face when we,
        his nephews and nieces, including Miss Mary,
    when we would say his name, Uncle Tom.

Yet certainly that embarrassment does appear to my generation,
    a positive sign maybe in our racial evolution,
but for me it is beyond disquieting to the point of rage,
    the sneer and snide comment his name engenders.
And if his name on my lips, Uncle Tom, causes you any jeer or snicker,
    whatever your race or sensibility,
then fuck you! and the horse you should have rode in on,
    but didn't…
because unlike Uncle Tom you don't know how to ride.

Unlocking Old Secrets

Uncle Tom is my father's older brother,
    by 18 months to be precise,
an ex-military man, a pilot of both fighters and bombers,
    and therefore a man as you might expect
    who does not tolerate foolishness well.

The two of us one day were riding horse on his huge ranch,
    a ranch that lays out near Sonoma in the Valley of the Moon,
    a gorgeous valley 2 hours north of San Francisco,
        (where Jack London delighted to live and write,
        just west of Napa Valley there over the mountains),
our not riding out amongst his horses and cattle,
    and him teaching me patiently how to lasso and rope,
but instead out amongst his orchards, checking water content,
    grapes and plums and pears and figs,
not only the water of the soil but the fruit as well,
    riding briskly for fun along the grape vines on the side of a foothill,
    each of us in a separate row,
        galloping occasionally just for the hell of it.

After maybe 30 minutes that day of listening to me on and off moan,
    whining over my first true love ever, a Columbiana I met in Mexico,
        (a special language course between semesters at SF State,
        immersed in a family environment in Guadalajara the both of us,
        and suddenly like a dream did I find myself immersed in beautiful her),
he finally pulled his beloved bay Rodrigo to a halt in a row of grapes,
    and turned him towards me, a row downslope from him.

        "Suck it up, Stevie," he demanded, looking across the grapes. "For God sakes, suck it up. This won't be the hardest thing in your life, not by a long shot. Just get over it, Squirt."

He did still take a little time to console me.
　　My heart broken, he told me, especially in a foreign country,
　　would only make me heartier…just get done with it.
After all, he said, you're not a high schooler any more,
　　you're in college now…act like you belong there.

I asked him with a mild undertone of 'so's-your-mother'
　　if he had had girlfriends in England during the war,
　　and did he have one just turned sour on him,
　　　　and the memory of it like hugging a porcupine,
　　as had my first love, me and that lovely Columbiana,
　　　　our relationship destroyed by her family and friends,
　　　　　　(and of course by our lack of experience,
　　　　　　not to mention the entire situation in Mexico
　　　　　　something as a whole foreign to the both of us),
　　　　and he looked down at me, eye to eye,
　　　　man to man actually,
　　　　　　perhaps the first time ever,
　　telling me things now never told before.

Indeed he had, he said, with a beautiful woman named Heloise,
　　not his first time in England, flying fighters in the Battle of Britain,
　　　　(and tales of that thrilling me, Neil, and Erik as kids),
　　but the second time returning and flying B-17 bombers.

Now would I learn of it, and not Neil nor Erik, the tales untold,
　　how the proud captain of a Flying Fortress and a leader of men,
　　arrived in England knowing little to nothing really about women and war,
　　　　even though he had flown Hurricanes in the Battle of Britain,
　　but on his departure that second time from England
　　　　was he savvied sorrowfully and devastated,
　　　　spiritually crushed by the horror of war,
　　and broken hearted by the dark side of passion

Hurricanes, Spitfires, and the Black Knight

Uncle Tom told me that when he first arrived in England,
    Spitfires were the only plane on his mind,
      the center piece of every air battle fought,
        bringing down that German aerial Armada;
but after his assignment to Hurricanes he soon learned the truth,
    that what Spitfires did mostly was shield those Hurricanes,
and shield them well they did from those deadly dark Messerschmitts,
    all black and fearful, those Messerschmitts,
      except for their signature yellow cowling,
        so bright on the nose, so seeable in the sky,
the Messerschmitt the fastest, the most weaponized of all warplanes,
    not only machine guns in each wing but a cannon in that nose,
      brilliantly in synch to the rotation of the propeller,
        its spitting booming death and destruction impossibly,
        right through the hub of its propeller blades,
and the Messerschmitt truly the deadliest plane in the sky,
    known amongst the Brits indeed as the Black Knight,
and no British pilot in his bad dreams and nightmares
    who did not see that yellow beaked bastard,
      coming right at him bloodthirsty and ruthless,
just like the Black Knight in King Arthur legends.

And the Spitfire's duty in those daily battles
    was to hold that Black Knight at bay,
while the Hurricanes did the dirty work,
    coming down like hawks on the Heinkel bombers,
      if hawks could spit deadly bloody flames
    and bring those eagles down crashing,
      leaving dangling men in the sky,
        sometimes on fire.

On the ground the Spitfires were treated like Ferraris,
    and the Hurricanes like pick-up trucks on a farm—
      the vehicle that delivered the goods,
the Spitfire pilots getting the pride and the glory,
    like the cavalry in years gone by,
While the Hurricanes were the infantry, the grunts, the spear-chuckers,
and for kills the Spitfires got red swastikas painted brightly on fuselage,
    while the Hurricane got a bomb for each Heinkel brought down,
and that did gall Uncle Tom some, his pride.

The Spitfires were the knights all right,
    and it stuck a bit in his craw,
especially when the Battle for Britain suddenly was over,
    and that not known by white flag or ceremony or surrender,
    but only known because the Germans just stopped coming,
        first one day none, then none the next…and the next…and then the next,
    and Goering rumored to have fled France in his powder blue uniform,
        returning to Germany, cursing, failed by his Luftwaffe,
            (what a vicious, strutting, murdering jackass he must have been).

The Spitfire pilots were lauded,
while the Hurricane men gratefully thanked,
    especially in the gut wrenching speech of Churchill,
        (Never in the field of human conflict
        so much owed… by so many…to so few,
and the same could be said by the world as a whole,
    never so much by so many to so few.

They were the knights all right, the Spitfire pilots,
    and that stuck like I said in Uncle Tom's craw,
        or so he told me,
    a man who from his boyhood days,
        in both high school and college too,
    was always the hero and used to being one,
    and right then he did not really consider himself such,
        when leaving England that first time coming home,
but he thought it was because of the Spitfire glory,
    not realizing then that no one with any humanity at all
    returns home from war thinking himself a hero.

Return to England

Two years later in 1942 he would return,
    both to England and to Heloise,
returning as a pilot and captain of a B-17, the Flying Fortress,
    and truly by far the biggest, most powerful plane in the sky.
And Uncle Tom as the pilot and 24 year old captain of his 17,
    it was his place and privilege to name that plane,
        the one in which he and his men would brave the skies,
            and maybe live, and maybe die;
and though most planes were named after women of varying virtue,
    from Picadilly Lilly to The Memphis Belle,
Uncle Tom's was not.

His plane he named The Scarlet Knight,
    come to England with tactics of daylight bombing,
        the 17's so powerful they boasted no need for fighter support,
    just tight formation and their dozen guns blazing,
        plus a motorized ball turret gunner to protect its belly,
    and fuck you, you yellow-beaked Black Knight bastard,
        fuck you and that dark horse you rode in on.

But so quickly were they to learn such arrogance a deadly delusion,
    for Jerry was little if not resourceful and able,
and not a single Jerry not courageous in the sky;

and Flying Fortress was like a vaulted bank,
    and no bank built that cannot be robbed,
    especially in this case with head-on tactics,
        called 'Shwere punkt' by Jerry,
power assault at the point of weakness;

and soon Uncle Tom found himself head on into that malevolence,
    The Scarlet Knight and The Black Knight face to face and colliding,
    mission after mission head-on at each other,
    nearly 600 hundred miles per hour closing speed,
        guns and cannons blazing away,
        day after day after day…..

(Excerpt from The Journal of Taranis the Helvetian)

LEGEND OF THE NIGHTHORSE
(As Told by Tam)

Shagone

Among the Akatani is a legend I would soon learn,
   a legend told me by one of the horse trainers,
   a limping man named Tam wearing an Akatani torc,
      a torc of silver of the Lepanto tribe,
         a tribe that honors the wolf and the full moon.

In Akatani language, as in Gallic and Helvetian,
   dawn is Shagone, the goddess, beloved sister of Sequana,
and unlike sunset, especially among the Akatani,
   is dawn a divinity, not an event,
      a divine personage each morning embracing us all
         with love and light, seen or unseen, clear day or stormy,
   and bestowing upon us all freedom from the night.

Peculiar only to the Akatani language is Awendor, the Nighthorse,
   a breed cursed by Sequana eternally into darkness,
and itself a breed dark as a moonless night,
   from forelock to tail, from mane to fetlock,
nearly impossible to see without squint in the dark.

A Nighthorse lives in those dark and dense forests
   and hides during daylight in caves and stone grottoes,
   or under thick trees that permit no sunlight,
for the moment a Nighthorse takes embrace of Shagone
   is the moment a Nighthorse bursts entirely into flames.

What to humans is awesome and beautiful, Shagone,
   is devastation to Awendor, The Nighthorse,
making the creature mysterious and furtive,
   living a lonely life in terror of the dawn.

Zhan

Lived once a human child, according to this tale,
   born by her mother's volition in the waters of Zhanadón,
the Purple River of Akatania, the river source of Sequana,
   where she comes to seek her solitude and restore her divinity,
and therefore is a child born in those waters beloved to Sequana,
   and the name given this child by her mother was Zhan.

In a dense forest near Zhan's home,
   and a short ride from the Purple River,
lived an Awendor, a Nighthorse, a filly,
   her midnight blackness broken only by a watcheye,
     her left eye, a blue eye, as blue as the sea.

As Zhan grew to a child of 12, tall and slender,
her hair red as Shagone, she learned from her father
   the existence of the Awendor in the forest close by,
but unlike her father she had never seen the dark creature
   because after dark never was she allowed into the forest,
   where howling wolves lived who hunted solely at night.

     "But what about the Awendor," she cried, "her alone with the wolves in the night?"

     "Don't you worry about her," her father assured her. "Never lived a wolf could outrun a Nighthorse."

Zhan learned from her mother the curse of the Nighthorse,
   cursed because once in a time long ago,
proud and prancing in their shiny sheen blackness,
   with sudden exuberance one dawn seeing Shagone on horizon,
a herd of them frolicking had on accident
   trampled to death a human lad who loved them,
     a lad also born of the purple waters of Zhanadón,
     and therefore beloved of Sequana;
   and Sequana, filled with anger, cursed them and said,

"Black as you are, you shall live only by night,
   and will live your lives in loneliness,
     except just for the Solstice of Winter,
when for those few hours in brevity
   in the sunlight you may cavort;
but when night falls your loneliness resumes
   and back into the dark—the Nighthorse."

Awendor and Zhan

Zhan grew tall and slender, and red-headed,
   and even at 12 was she strong of hand and wrist.
     from daily milking her father's cows in the dairy,
   and strong of arms and shoulder
     from daily churning butter and cheese for her mother,
the strongest milkmaid, said her father with pride,
   even stronger than her mother as maid;
and her mother agreed, giving Zhan great pride,
   which consoled her heart, for as an only child,
     was she lonely as the Nighthorse.

Then happened one night because of her loneliness,
   unable to sleep and Shagone drawing near,
she rose up while her parents were sleeping
   rose up and walked near the forest.

Though warned many times of the wolves in the night,
she was drawn there mysteriously by thought of Awendor,
   yet listened there prudently for any howling to flee.

The same color as the hair of this slender child,
   the glow of Shagone on this moonless night
     barely exceeded the starlight above the horizon
when Zhan heard something unexpected,
   not howling nor baying but whinnying instead,
     and snorting and the rumbling sounds of a struggle;
and drawing near a pit outside the edge of the forest,
   a pit made by movement of the earth many lifetimes before,
she saw Awendor, the Nighthorse, trapped down in the dark.

Zhan understood at once the Nighthorse in her loneliness
    had come out of the forest in the darkness seeking,
and having never known the danger of treeless pits,
    had quickly fallen prey to one in a night without moon.

In the faint glow of Shagone Zhan felt desperate the Awendor,
    and heard sounds of her leaping and snorts of her pain,
    front hooves barely reaching the top of the pit
and pounding for hold in the soft moistened soil,
    but each time slipping back down in the dark,
for Zhan saw now around the edge of the pit
    the marks each time where hooves had dug deep,
and yet each time had failed and sunk back.

On the top of the pit Zhan stood now and heard from below
    huge whinnying bellow and she gasped in dread
when hooves from the darkness pounded suddenly at her feet,
    clubbing and digging into soft soil there;
and Zhan now saw the dark muzzle of Awendor
craning neck to escape the fire when glow of Shagone
    comes soon breaking light beams brightly over the horizon.

Zhan was frightened down to the depth of her heart,
frightened by the sound and fury of Awendor desperate,
    and would have shrunk back from the pit
    or perhaps even have fled in fear,
but that left eye of the Nighthorse,
    blue as the sea even dim in the glow,
that watcheye fell on her, earnest in plea,
and instantly Zhan reached forward her love,
    seizing the mane in one hand strong from milking
    and neck with arm and shoulder fibered by churning,
and pulled with her strength, all her love from within,
falling backwards and down as she pulled on the Nighthorse.
    It was enough.
    It was bridged.

Up from the pit rose the Nighthorse in glistening magnificence,
    as light broke far over horizon and bright,
but desperate in heart to flee horror of fire,
    she trampled over Zhan, all hooves on the child,
        breaking bones of her pelvis and one of left leg.

Through her fetlocks and legs
Awendor had felt crack of the child's bones
    and turned her head back in the breaking of light,
    her blue eye upon the red child who had saved her,
but already she felt the burn piercing her hide
    and turning she abandoned the child, galloping away,
        the morning light chasing her as she fled, but blocked
            long enough by the trees of the dense and dark forest
            for Awendor to flee into a stone covered grotto
                and pass the day urgently in the safety of shadows,
                then hurry that night to the edge of the forest
            to look for the girl who had wrapped arms around her;
but when she did so,
    and the many nights thereafter,
was there no sign of that child,
    no sign who had saved her,
the girl with red hair
    as red as Shagone.

Zhan's Agony

After she fell and was trampled by Awendor desperate,
    and had watched the filly turn back her blue eye before fleeing,
Zhan thought she had heard the wolves howling,
    and in agony had she crawled herself desperately home.

Over the next weeks and months of pain, though carted
    daily by her loving mother to the Purple River
    and washed by loving hands in Sequana's waters,
Zhan healed neither quickly nor well;
    and her mother eventually lost hope
        not only in Sequana's benevolence,
        but also in Zhan's future to ever bear child,
    and ceased carting her daughter to The Purple River,
    in disillusion and deep despair.

With great struggle throughout that year of tears,
   Zhan learned to walk again.
Whenever her own hopes had dwindled failing,
   she remembered the Nighthorse leaping again and again
      until the sound and fury of struggle
      brought salvation to the edge of that pit,
   and Zhan remembered the Nighthorse in dark magnificence
      rising up from the pit and turning blue eye in gratitude
      then fleeing perforce before holocaust into the darkness.

Remembering her thus buoyed Zhan's spirit and heart.

After a year of such struggle and with stick in hand
   she could walk well enough to do chores as before,
      to strengthen again her hands in milking
      and her arms again and shoulders fibered by churning,
   and nightly she listened to wolves howling in the forest
      and feared for the Nighthorse alone in the dark.
Her father again told her do not fret,
   and again said with nodding assurance and his calming hands,

        "Never lived a wolf could outrun a Nighthorse,
        never, not one, nor a pack of them ever."

Zhan's Quest

Came a day Zhan decided herself again strong enough,
   and that same night, a long night, a night full of moon,
in blue cloak she wrapped herself and her hair red as Shagone,
   in cloak as blue as the watcheye of Awendor,
and with walking stick in hand and parents asleep,
   listening intently for distant howling of wolves,
   into the forest she went in search of Awendor,
to see the filly's face and blue eye again in the moonlight,
   or know the silence of her bones.

From her father she had understanding of stars and lunar path
   and could find her way home by backtrack of the moon,
   and would do so instantly at the near howling of wolves.

But the night came cloudy and the forest pitch black,
    and though she tried to stay on path of the stars,
    when clouds cleared a 2nd time before the face of the moon,
        she realized that in the dark
        she had lost track of the heavens.
Hearing no howling she began calling, "Awendor, Awendor,"
    and grew more and more desperate
    as moon sunk and Shagone neared.

In dark total desperation, she called "Awendor" loudly,
    the clouds clearing a 3rd time before the face of the moon,
and then she heard the soft whinny of the Nighthorse close by,
    and turning she saw her standing in a moonlit grotto.

So black was she that even in the moonlight
    only her blue eye was certain to see;
and with broad smile and walking stick
    Zhan limped toward the Nighthorse.

Awendor had seen and remembered the red girl limping
    and knew the why of it as much as any horse can know.
Now she too walked toward the other, head lowered
    in gratitude and sorrow as much as any horse can show,
and from the girl's touch sensed no bitterness nor anger
    and felt the girl's heart as much as any horse can feel.
The girl even put her hands on Awendor's muzzle, lifting it,
    and withdrew from her blue cloak a delicious sweet apple,
as sweet as any apple Awendor ever had known.

After letting the Nighthorse take the apple,
    Zhan put arm around her muzzle and face
and put ear to her cheek just below the watcheye,
    listening with pleasure to the crunch and chew gently
    as the Nighthorse delighted in the sweet fruit, and nodding.

From that moment on were they as one heart.

Flight

It was then,
    as the Nighthorse swallowed the last sweet morsel,
it was then Zhan realized themselves surrounded,
    eyes of crafty wolves stealthily upon them in the night,
but wary of hooves and slow to assault.

Taken by the presence of the girl limping in the moonlight
    Awendor had not sensed their creep nor wild scent.
At command of instinct she turned to gallop and flee,
    but heard the voice of the girl again,
        "Awendor, Awendor, do not leave me."

The Nighthorse turned back instantly, back to Zhan,
    the child with hair as red as Shagone—
She would not abandon her a second time.

Zhan threw down the walking stick
    and scrambled up on her back,
    and they were off in a gallop,
        as the wolves closed in
        and Shagone drew near.

Never lived a wolf could outrun a Nighthorse.

High soaring, Awendor leapt over the pack leader
    who rolled and hunkered to dodge her hard hooves.
Even more than the wolves
    she knew every tree in the forest,
and with Zhan leaning forward head to head,
    grasping mane and withers with firm hands,
    her strong arms and shoulders securing her balance,
    enduring the pain in bones of pelvis and leg,
did the Nighthorse now gallop under limbs of the trees,
galloped just ahead of the howling wolves,
    galloping with the burden of the child on her back,
and galloped to the edge of the forest and beyond.

With the glow of Shagone now come on horizon,
    and her blue watcheye focused with piercing intent
out of the forest she galloped, wolves at her fetlocks,
    and leapt with ease the pit that once had ensnared her,
    bearing the girl who had saved her, red hair long in the wind.

"Zhanadón," cried the girl reaching out her left hand;
"Zhanadón," holding fingers to cheek below the blue eye;
"Zhanadón," and turned muzzle due west the Purple River
    and the mercy of Sequana, sister of Shagone.
"Never a wolf," cried the girl. "Our fate is Zhanadón."

Awendor galloping heard the howling of the wolves
    running now close to surely outflank her,
    seeing her slowed by her burden of child,
and on her flesh she felt streaky heat of faint light.

Now she knew in her heart, as much as any horse can know,
    could be no turning back.
Now she strove harder at heart than any horse can strive
    to carry the girl safely to the faintly seen river,
there to plunge her surely into its sheltering darkness
    before came the light
    and her own burst into flames.

Zhan too on her legs could feel the heat rising
    and called into the ear of the Nighthorse galloping,
        "You are Awendor, heart of my heart.
        Leap us both now into the Purple River,
        two as one now into Zhanadón."

With the last of her effort as the howling closed in
    and the light broke full over the crimson horizon,
Awendor the Nighthorse gave mighty leap from bank of the river
    and burst into flames like a shooting star in the sky
    and plunged the girl safely into those dark waters,
        The Purple River of Sequana, beloved Zhanadón,
    Zhan crying out to the unseen goddess,
    "Awendor has saved me,
        heart of my heart.
    Awendor has saved me
        in light of Shagone."

Sequana's Decree

The ways of the gods are unknown to men,
the only certainty is that the gods are moved
   not by tearful supplication and bended plea,
   but by courage and sacrifice among men.

So it was in that morning sun
   that Sequana heard Zhan's voice crying out,
and the waters of Zhanadón, the Purple River,
   welcomed them both,
      the crippled child and the Nighthorse who bore her,
     healing the child, restoring her to fullness;
and when with child still safe on her back
   Awendor the Nighthorse rose from purple waters,
     into the brilliant light of Shagone,
   they both saw immediately the change.

Where in the light she had burst into flame
was now fully healed and red roan in color,
   like the morning sun bright on the horizon,
   or the hair of the child saved by her great heart,
but still midnight black were mane and withers,
   forelock and tail, and all four legs,
     fetlocks to hooves.

So did the Nighthorse everywhere by Sequana's decree
   suddenly each find itself changed in color
and welcomed again in the morning light,
   a new breed named by Zhan's mother gladly,
   now known as Zhagandór, to honor
      two great hearts,
      the waters that bore them,
      and the light they now prance in,
      and frolic.

Final Thought

When I first heard this legend of the Nighthorse
    from the Akatani horse trainer Tam,
I thought it a bit of honey bread,
    sweet to those who have a taste for it.

But I would soon live that legend, in essence,
    the heart of it,
with the Zhagandór who chose me
    to be her horseman,
Veranya her name, and like with Zhan,
    soon would 2 hearts become as one…

Excerpt from HighPockets and the Blue Guitar)

Killing the Old Nazi

Prologue

Several times in training, me and Widow,
  we talked of good and evil,
though mostly was Widow hostile to the subject,
  not so much disagreeing as just somehow angry.

Of God and spirit, he acknowledged the possibility,
  especially spirit, no anathema there.
Something there is he agreed whole-heartedly,
  something that moves us beyond flesh and blood.
But any talk of God he found suspicious, even insulting,
  and in fact rarely said 'God' but 'Infinitude' instead.

It was not mocking God, Infinitude, not at all,
  although his totally up in the air about Divinity,
but instead mocking was he the people think they know,
  those absolutely certain of the mind of God
  and quite willing to tell you all about it,
  or even terrorize you, some of them,
    for the good of your own soul of course,
  a stance caused high dudgeon in both me and Widow,
and corrupt priests too, he said, them especially—
  (big news story breaking that week about pedophile priests,
  and woe unto them, alive or dead, if the Monsignor had his way).

For all of them did Widow create Infinitude,
  and comic it was how it stung those pretenders to the quick,
    (but not Rez who found it funny yet respectful).

Never had I spoken to Widow about Walter Jürgens,
  about all that Expo experience, mundane and Divine.
Not that it was a case of pearls before swine,
  not that at all—for other Marines maybe but not for Widow,
and really more a case of waiting for the right moment.

Cherry-Breakers

In Paraguay our first adventure lay,
   our absolute first mission and trek,
   the cherry-breaker as Harlot Moors call it,
even though Colonel Mooring hated that—
   (in his mind it meant his men getting fucked),
and therefore never said in his presence,
   or he'd dress you down like a raw recruit,
   and I'm here to tell you that's a hard truth.

Out in the bush of Paraguay were we and on our own,
   dropped off by an army Huey, our last touch of the civilized,
   and think on that— an army Huey your last touch,
the army needed because of this mission's urgency,
3 days from Harlot Moors notified to mission execution, including travel,
   and one day's strategy session in Mariscal,
   and then the long Huey ride to drop-off point.

There we were, well northwest of Asuncion,
   well west of the Paraguay river, huge from Brazil,
our trek to take us east through bush to the edge of grasslands,
   first to a fast moving river comes off the that huge Paraguay,
      not a tributary to it but a no-return from it,
      one of its rare no-returners and therefore a bit swift;
and then on further east our trek, in heat and sapping humidity,
   coming out of the bush, crossing over a wide creek,
   out into some very green and lush grass lands,
and that's where we'd find him, his remote house and grounds,
   there at the base of the 'Long Gone' hills, or so Intel called them,
   his pretty much living there remote all these years since the war,
and access only by 4-wheeler or helicopter, *(or trained scout-sniper),*
   a land once owned and farmed by Mennonites,
      (believe it or not, a colony of them in Paraguay many years),
and whether they moved on or were murdered by this old Nazi,
   we had no idea, none at all, nor did it matter now,
for there had he been all these years since the war.

When we had met the Huey pilots at the takeoff strip,
   one black, one Asian,
both me and Widow were already by orders in paint and Ghillie suits,
   no armor at all, nor flak jackets, nothing like that,
     only quickness, 9-Mikes, Ghillies and face paint to protect us,
       and my M-40 in canvas bag on my back,
         to be assembled once we reached the target,
       and our Ghillies fashioned for both bush or grassland camouflage;
and suited up like that, me and Widow, face paint and Ghillies,
   we kind of made the young Huey pilots giggle.

But those were our orders, fully suited up completely at takeoff,
   and that done to maintain our anonymity;
not that this mission broke International Law,
but it was dark gray for Paraguay for sure,
   this old Nazi protected among others
     by someone up high in their government,
       (and only for dollars not politics at this late date),
and him an old Nazi not likely our killing him
   would stir up much international protest,
but still we had Marine paranoia,
   what we called Corps Values,
and anonymity the better part of valor here.

Also because of our paranoia and those Corps Values
these pilots had just gotten their orders that morning,
   a long flight over bush and jungle,
     (for them a hazard they shunned if they could),
   and neither of them any way pleased by that ride,
but still they really did giggle seeing us.

      "Which one's the black man," said the black pilot, there beside
      the Huey.

         (The Asian copilot pointed at me
         all of us standing on the tarmac.)

"Must be him," he said. "He's the dumbest looking of the two."

"Hey," said Widow, "what the fuck are *you* saying?"

"Relax," said the copilot. "Nothing personal. I'm just punking *him*."

"When you think about it," I said, "it's really an anti-racist joke, the white guy actually being the stupid looking one, kinda like inscrutable *Chin* here," —that last said at him with some bite and accusing thumb.

Widow liked that and we bumped fists,
   the copilot accepting it as his due,
but their edginess obvious, no attempt to hide it,
   their out of the blue thrust into that jungle,
   or at least over it, and a long distance too.

Then me and Widow took a long look at each other,
   and that started us laughing at our own selves,
      Ghillie suits and face paint all over us on cement and tarmac,
      really kind of comical if you think about it,
      like beached hammerheads wrapping themselves in seaweed to hide;
but in the bush were those suits and paints so well-crafted
   that if we lost sight of each other,
   we could not find each other,
      not without shouting.

         "Who you gonna be? I said and Widow banged my fist,
         the constant shout from Colonel Mooring in training.

It was a long loud flight, plugs in our ears,
   the occasional drip of hydraulic fluid from the rotor,
and we could see them both at the controls dead serious alert,
   looking at the eternal jungle and bush below us;
and it certainly made them nervous,
   their constantly checking and looking at their maps on clipboards,
   like an obsession to be absolutely certain they were on course,
and ritually tapping their instruments for malfunction as we flew,
   taking no chance of forced down into that nightmare jungle,
then total relief on their faces their seeing the huge clearing,
turning to us and pointing at it, as if they had created it,
   10 kliks due south of the huge mount used for marker.

Normally we'd repel down from the Huey into the jungle,
    but not this time by strategy.
Instead they dropped us into that pre-arranged clearing,
    not even setting the Huey down, just hovering,
them afraid that jungle somehow like the Blob
    would up and seize them and suck them down;
and that forced us to jump out knee high above the soft ground,
    us in those Ghillie suits and all,
an unnecessary risk of ankle injury, though a minor one,
    which angered Widow far more than me,
and him cussing them as they whirled and hightailed it home.

And a long trek it was for us to the target,
    to absolutely guarantee no US connection to this killing;
but at least we were dropped off on time,
    20 kilometers from the target,
    a 2 day trek through that bush and heat and back,
our relying totally first day on my land-nav,
    which pretty much for that mission meant
    holding the compass in my left hand
    and just running straight ahead into the sun…
        well, maybe not quite that simple.

The need for urgency was huge to make this mission happen,
    this old Nazi riddled with cancer throughout his body,
    and the fear he'd be dead before anybody could shoot him;
and thus the reason the Mossad reached out to us,
    this Nazi only recently uncovered by informant,
    and their vehement passion he not die in his bed—
no asset of their own available and trained to act so quickly,
    only us, the Harlot Moors, and no doubt huge
    the favor they either called in or gave,
but unfortunately that urgency afforded us only
    a single session of strategy before departure.

After 30 minutes or so into the jungle,
 time to test to satisfaction the fit and function of our Ghillie suits,
we shed them gladly because of the humidity,
 and folded them and packed them on each other's back,
 no way we could cover ground quickly wearing them,
 too cumbersome, too hot and way too sweaty,
and even in fatigue shirts and floppy head cover
still we had to hydrate near constantly as we went,
 sipping from the spout of our camelbacks strapped to our shoulders,
 each of us encouraging the other to hydrate.

 "Who you gonna be?" we called to each other.

That first night were we to reach that no-return river,
 one of the few, like I say, that actually drained from the Paraguay,
 and thus fairly fast moving it was, but not knock down swift,
and the next day would be 12 kliks to the target's farmhouse.

Now truly were me and Widow depending on each other,
 isolated and alone in snake-infested Paraguay,
 our totally under assault by savage bush reality,
  as if we were the only 2 people now alive on the planet,
   thrown into the opposite of the Garden of Eden,
    that kind of onliness;
and each of us absolutely with an eye on the other,
 an overwhelming apprehension seizing us,
 very much like the coil of a giant anaconda,
for if you found yourself all alone in that bush—
 that meant certain death for sure.

Near constant were the sounds of course,
 from tropical bird sounds just like the movies,
 to wind in the trees and dripping things,
  and other sounds, including some things animal,
  but we never encountered anything dangerous.

Another thing, nothing prepares your nose for tropical smells,
 truly an assault of odors, stinks, and scents in the bush,

although may be a delightful smell of a tropical flower momentarily,
    but followed in seconds by revolting dead carcass stench;
and the bush is rough, not like leaves of grass,
    but stuff that can reach out and tear your fatigues,
        even a Ghillie suit when you're in one,
    and then your own flesh, needles and thorns,
and infection in the bush near deadly as a Tommy Goff,
    (one of a dirty dozen of deadly vipers and serpents).
Oh yeah, the Garden of Eden.

Far more than the old Nazi and his security guards
    snakes were our number one adversary,
        not to mention Brown spiders and their Hobo kin,
so deadly were they, especially so many of these slitherers,
    that sometimes all you had post bite was minutes to half an hour—
        and then a very rough good-by.
Fer-de-Lance or tropical rattler or even the deadlier Tommy Goff,
    you can just pick your poison literally,
        though Tommy Goffs unlikely this far south,
            or so the book said, but everyone knew
                that the Marine Manual just like Scripture,
                      full of some very bad science.

By strategy, and very unusual, Widow carried no M-16,
    the only rifle my sniper M-40 in its canvass case on my back,
and no armor or flak jacket either of us, none at all,
    speed not security our number one strategy,
        as well as our not sweating ourselves dry in that humidity,
            ergo our constant hydrating as we moved,
            and more than a handful of salt and chlorine tablets,
the both of us with our 9-Mikes and Ka-bar knives handy,
    one in a holster right side on our belts, safety off,
    the other newly sharpened in a sheath on the left.

9-Mikes in that bush were better than rifles,
and that for a very simple and obvious reason—
    any danger would be up close and personal,
        and totally relying on reflex action,
    and my reflexes world class quick as Widow knew
    made him comfortable enough someone else on lead;

and rhino, crock, grizzly bear, lion or tiger, or man,
    a 9-Mike auto will down it before you empty your clip,
        assuming all your shots well placed in a tight pattern,
        which means right down the gullet or throat,
            or 5 in the chest of an upright bear,
            or back of the head of an angry crock,
                (just watch out for your legs).
Snakes we'd just use our Ka-bar to sever the head.

Also isolating us was our total radio silence,
    command not wanting anyone picking up American chatter,
    and then connecting that chatter to the dead Nazi,
        our only to send code first night reaching the river,
        and then second night back to the river safely,
    even changing our usual code just to be certain,
        using an alternative I came up with myself,
    including our mission call sign— "Tommy Goff,"
        just because of that snake scaring the piss out of me.
That's when the Intel guy said no Tommy Goff that far south.

        "Sez who?" I had said.

        "Sez the book."

        "And you believe the book word for word."

        "Always," he said.

                (He said that faking a man insulted,
                which meant I had made my point.)

In our study of snakes that strategy day, especially Paraguay,
    we for sure had studied that Tommy Goff,
but also the corals and their non-venomous look-a-likes,
which took some time to differentiate one from another—
    a good bluff if you've got no deadly squirting fangs
    to just dress and act like a local vicious killing gangster,
        especially those red rings around you,
    so no one *not* deadly will take any chance with you.

Our prime directive was just don't get caught,
   the old Nazi down to 3 security guards and dogs,
and all of them bargain-basement,
   and pretty much bored to tears,
   never before any assault on this old Geezer.

No problem we were told, no problem with any of them,
   just to use our heads and follow training.

      "But what about those guards?" Widow had said.

      "They're players too," said the Intel Captain. "Take 'em out if you have to, but only them. The rest are domestics and a nurse. They are not players. But not security, they *are* players *and* they are blood, and if they threaten or even just interfere, take 'em out."

Crossing That River of No Return

That first night we lay beside that gurgling river,
   our first marker achieved and message sent,
and let me tell you, at night the bush is loud with insects,
   and occasionally something like a growl or the like,
   or a crack of something falling in the brush,
but that total insect buzz and sound at night,
   and you'll not believe this,
it sounds so much like Christmas sleigh bells,
   counterpoint to that river gurgling so close by us,
15 or so merry sleighs constantly circling you jingling.

Isolated as we were in that creepy, dangerous world,
now were me and Widow truly feeling each other out,
   our having already crossed that river so as not to in the morning,
      both of us embarrassed on our crossing
         by the huge blunder each of us had made in the river.

Fast moving like I said but not truly knock down swift,
   and only about 5 feet deep where we chose to cross,
      (that choice having been Widow's responsibility),
still it was steady current and demanded attention,
   and surprised me how chilly it was in that heat.

Also in the tropics are parasites sometimes in the water,
    and very aggressive little critters are they,
which is why you don't piss waist deep in the water,
    because they'll find their way right up your urine stream,
    hustling quick as they can right into your peter,
and in a couple of hours Ol' Peter's the size of Paul Bunyan's,
    and that's a Peter and Paul experience nobody cares for.

They say can even happen just pissing from a bank,
    but really that's just a myth to scare Cherry-Breakers,
a myth like water swirling counterclockwise south of the equator.

Both of us when fording, holding our gear and Ghillies overhead,
    Widow being especially careful with comm equipment,
    and me with my M-40 held high in its canvas bag,
        (all equipment stowed in watertight bags,
        but on your own in the bush you just never know);
and first me, I stumbled stupidly on a rock,
    and down to one knee I went, struggling in the current,
    head and floppy under, and water up my nose.

Widow moved quickly to help me,
    but just as quickly was I back on my feet,
perhaps my urgency pricked by a fear of snakes in the water,
    (and also scary those parasites finding their way up my nose),
and only me going under and not the equipment,
    but me back on my feet quickly gave Widow space to hoot.

> "Come on, shooter," he said, "do you need me throwing you over my shoulder?"
>
> "That'll be the day."
>
>   *(I was hugely embarrassed.)*

Karma or not Widow took 3 steps and stumbled,
    just as if I had tripped him,
exactly the same as me, head and floppy under,
    gear, Ghillie, and comm equipment held safe overhead,
and also exactly as me scrambled quickly to his feet,
    him more afraid of parasites than snakes.

At first I entertained the thought Widow had fallen on purpose,
   just so I wouldn't feel such an ass,
but on the riverbank both of us soaking,
   he swore that was not the case.

Just a couple of stank ass cherry-breakers, he said,
   and him truly embarrassed like me to the core,
tripping over our own feet, no threat in our faces.

      "Cherry-breakers or stank ass," I said cheerfully, "that river water cleaned us right up."

      (My nose now seemed cleansed by that river,
      and all smells had taken on fresh experience.)

      "How can we be any more rookie than that," groaned Widow, us now up on the dirt bank stomping off river water, "falling on our ass first time in the river."

      (Where we stood was one of the few places along the river
      where green groundcover and foliage did not reach out
      and cover the entire banks, not this side nor the other,
      where were scattered rocks all around in the dirt,
      some 10 million year old geologic oddity,
      never before witnessed by human beings.)

      "Think of it as baptism," I said, "a couple of Dunkards going under."

      "I got your baptism," he said. "I got it right here."

      (He had his hand at his crotch).

      "And here's me thinking you done it so I wouldn't feel such a shithead."

      "And there's you still thinking like a cherry-breaker."

Setting Up Camp

That night we lay beside the river of nasty current,
    no fire set of course or needed actually in that heat,
and we listened to the splash and gurgle of the river,
    and the constant jingle bell jangle of insects,
    and mostly out of training habit we whispered.

Because of the snakes and critters and skeeters after dark,
    and other dangers as well by a river,
we were thoroughly sheathed in our Ghillie wraps and hoods,
    fully clothed and sweaty of course and our faces barely seen.

Normally in the field Harlot Moors sleep back to back,
    your pistol handy with safety on,
but in the savage wild backwater of Paraguay,
    (no single place in the civilized world where
    that old Nazi felt safe enough to die in his bed),
there we slept face to face,
    a short wall of rocks around our heads and nylon netting over us,
        like the curved wall of some small shrine, the rocks,
        and the camouflage netting, one edge under the rocks,
    and raised by 2 sticks we had snatched along our trek,
        reaching up just about a foot or so above the rocks,
    and down then like a ski jump past our feet and fastened there by pegs,
    so if some snake or critters tried to climb up the rocks,
        they will be deflected down and away from us;
    and luckily neither Widow nor me much given to snoring,
        but that night we did do some talking.

Most guys on a mission only talk mission,
    and nothing else but mission,
no wives, no family, no good friends,
    no nothing, just total business 24/7.

But that was not our way, me and Widow,
    especially not on this first mission,
        where our biggest fear was jungle not people,
and our realizing we hardly knew each other,
    even after all the training we'd been through.

At first we did talk about this mission itself,
    both of us feeling some reservation first hearing it,
    even after we were explained the Mossad urgency,
but our main reservation was the target, a tottering old man,
    him in his last days, a week or 2 at most to live.
He may be blood, we had said, but long since from player,
    and how possibly does this save life?

Colonel Mooring had shown us the documentation,
    telling us we had the right of refusal on this one,
but understand this, he had said, and understand it well—
    this is a former chief of guards at Treblinka,
    and well documented are his grisly murders,
        not only adults but children too,
            (and we saw it all in the documents and photos).

A man does that, said Colonel Mooring, kills the innocent,
    then he's always a player, always blood, all his life.
You murder children, he said, and you're never not a player,
    and this will tell the world Justice prevails,
    absolutely, sooner or later, Justice prevails.

Me and Widow looked at each other,
    and in perfect unison nodded our heads.
No one like that should die in his bed—
    we both agreed and bumped our fists,
    a matter of Justice indeed,
and the documentation on this guy so massive
    no chance of treachery by the Mossad,
    absolutely none at all.
Who you gonna be, we said to each other.

Comrades Talking

So there we lay in the bush of Paraguay, still embarrassed,
   me and Widow feeling like a couple of stiffs from Hoboken,
   listening to the river gurgling its boast of taking both of us down,
and us realizing the 2 of us barely knowing each other,
   even after all we'd been through training and before.

Widow had just been to the edge of the bush and back,
   a scary experience your pants down in this savage wild,
so many killers out there all around you, big *and* small,
   and like those parasites in the river,
they *will* kill you if they can.

      "Ooo-eee, jim," Widow had proclaimed, "I just had me a righteous
      dump, a noble shit and now I'm feeling brave and magnificent
      and Ooo-eee I need to delve into things profound."

Even in the dim light I could see his broad grin and soaring satisfaction,
   and da Vinci laying down his brush last time from Mona Lisa,
   or Michelangelo climbing down last time from the ceiling,
neither could have been beaming any more broadly
   than Widow surviving pants down at night in this deadly wild.

That just goes to show you the truth about feelings,
   their substance and significance,
   not to mention reliability.
Feelings cannot tell you whether or not
   you have changed the world for everyone in it,
or just had for yourself that day dangerously
   an outstandingly healthy bowel movement.

      "When you think about it," he said, "we're gonna blow this old
      Nazi away tomorrow, so maybe we ought to have some deep
      thoughts about it."

      (Widow unlike me was a pure Liberal Arts major
      before he quit college and joined the Marines,
      and his father in fact a Professor of English literature,
      and unlike me Widow little exposure to math and science.)

"Why get your panties in a ruffle," I said, "you're not the one pulling the trigger."

*(Widow threw back his hood near violently,
rocking the netting some over our heads,
and went up on one elbow confronting me fiercely.)*

"Fuck you, Frisco. You're lucky I don't reach out and strangle you, you asshole, you shit bag, right there where you lay. You think you're doing this alone. You're not doing this alone. You don't do nothing alone unless I tell you to. We're a team, two faces on the same coin. One of us is nothing, not without the other. That guy dies tomorrow because of both of us, both of our decisions and not just yours. Pulling the trigger is the last thing we do, like turning out the lights before going home. We're a team, shithead. You hear me. Fuck you!"

*(I ripped back my own hood equally,
up on my elbow face-to-face, 6 inches apart,
my anger up and ready to confront,
but then relented after a moment's thought.)*

"You're right," I said, "There ain't no I in team."

"There ain't no asshole either."

"That guy dies tomorrow cause we're a team," I said. "Two rode together."

*(From out of my cape I now pulled my right hand.
Widow did the same except using his left,
struggling a little to throw off his cape.
We banged fists.)*

"Never say that to me again ever, Stevie."

"Never gonna happen," I said, "not who I'm gonna be."

(We covered and lay back down.)

"So a noble shit demands profundity," I said.

"Every time," he said, "every damn time. A little Plato please."

*(That bit of self-effacing made me laugh,
a liberal arts major, his always resolving to that.)*

"How about this," I said, "I have a theory about God."

"Take a number," he said.

"I'm serious, Widow. I think it's unique."

(He started to sniff at the air.)

"It's not bullshit," I said.

"Okay, tell me," he said, "but make it quick. It's vital to be quick when you're talking Infinitude. Please don't fucking bore me to tears either, not about that, not about Infinitude."

Quickly I explained my concept of God in Materialism,
   that water is God projecting His presence into material reality.
Water is the source of all cleansing, I said,
   both cherry-breaker or stank ass for example,
and the source of all healing, the source of all life,
   the source of all us,
the true source of all meaning in our existence.
Without water rock is the highest achievement of this universe.

"Does that rock include rhythm and blues?"

"Hey, I'm serious, humor me."

"Hardness is important," said Widow, "no doubt about *tha-a-at*."

"I'm talking granite hardness."

"I stand corrected, but ain't no granite around here."

"Yeah, you got that right," I said, "not around here. I never realized how soft the ground is in tropical bush."

"You got a finish for this idea," said Widow

(Came a huge buzzing and a big sag on our netting and Widow slapped hard at it, the back of a gloved hand.)

"Fuck me," I said, "was *that* a mosquito?"

"More like a flying tarantula," he said, himself a bit rattled.

(We both looked around ominously and then listened for a moment but heard only the river splashing and still gurgling its boast, and the constant sleigh bell jingle sounds of a million insects all around us.)

"Go ahead, finish," he said. "I think were safe."

"Without water," I continued, "there can be no life, not on this planet, and I predict no life anywhere in the universe. Water and light are the 2 keys to life and being, one the force and the other the receiver, and those are 2 of the 3 faces of God."

"You been thinking about this for a long time."

"Oh yeah, of course," I said.

"Keep going."

"Water for example is the total source of acid and alkaline, which is what creates life, the balance, the homeostasis, and you don't live long if your pH is not 7.4, the same as seawater I might point out."

"Really," said Widow, truly surprised by that fact of science.

"Oh yes, and one other thing— notice also that water, H_2O, is itself a trinity of a molecule. Just saying."

"What's the 3rd face?"

(Actually I kind of thought he'd laugh at me, and was mildly surprised that he did not, and that so pleased me I lost my train of thought.)

"The 3rd face?"

"Wake up, man. You got light, you got water. So tell me what's the 3rd face."

"Oh yeah— Spirit."

(Widow thought for a moment.)

"Which one's oxygen?"

"What?"

"You got H2O," said Widow, "the 3 faces of God. Which face is oxygen?"

"I don't know. I'd guess spirit."

"Guessing don't feed the bulldog, son."

"It's an analogy. Analogies break down."

"No, it's *not* an analogy," said Widow irritated. "What you got there is an explanation. Explanations are not allowed to break down."

"It's a work in progress."

"I never liked chemistry much," he said.

"I loved chemistry," I boasted, "and mathematics too."

"Oh stop," he said. "You're killing me here. Let's grab some sleep. Tomorrow's a big day for both of us."

"You're forgetting someone else too, aren't you?" I said.

"Not to mention him," said Widow.

Feeling safe enough now,
   the rock shrine around our heads,
   the nylon netting all over us,
     the constant insect jangle in the darkness,
we slept face to face our hoods cinched tight,
   pistols laying on rocks beside our heads,
   where we could reach them quickly if need be,
     their safeties off,
and our Ka-bars too right beside them in case of snakes.

Trek and Reverie

That second day went easy enough from the get-go,
   that first day's experience having initiated us some,
and now both of us squatted on the riverbank to wash,
   and then check each other's painted face.

"You missed a couple of spots," said Widow.

(With a quick swipe he painted a black line,
forehead down to the bridge of my nose,
and then a green one across both eyebrows,
an act that became a superstition for us,
and always those words, "you missed a spot.")

"First time, you know what they say," said Widow.

(He went to a knee beside me now,
reaching into the river to rinse his fingers.)

"No," I said, looking into the swift moving river, "I got no qualms about this guy. Every bit of me says this is pure justice."

(A last slap of water,
and up both of us stood.)

"Yeah, absolutely," he said, "this guy needs killing for sure. We can't let him just slip away back into the void thinking his last breath he beat the consequence."

(Standing there, hearing the river,
I looked right into Widow's face.)

"What if he did," I said to draw Widow out, "what if he did just die in his sleep. What difference does that make to anyone, to us, to you?"

"I don't care what it matters to anyone else, Stevie, it matters to me. We can't let this asshole escape what he did. Maybe it's only a moment when we kill him but he'll know. He'll know it cost him, what he did, even if it's only a couple of weeks. He'll *know* it cost him, and especially most where it counts the most, here at the end. He may be suffering but you notice he ain't gone and killed himself. Bet your ass there's a good reason for that. Guy's got something keeping him alive. Maybe only for an instant but he'll *know*."

(We reached down for our packs and slipped them over our shoulders, packs to be hooked to a drag line at destination.)

"Besides, we kill this guy, Stevie, and the word will go out, and old Nazis like him everywhere will know and tremble, and maybe all their last days just filled with fear. Justice is."

"I can live with that."

(I smiled and stuck out my fist.)

"To know and tremble," I said. "Who you gonna be?"

"Justice is," responded Widow, banging my fist.

(Now we turned our backs to the river and began our trek into the savage unknown.)

The trek was easy enough through bush and grassland,
    and it took us several hours, mostly in silence,
        our eyes alert of course for hazards and dangers,
            not only for critters but false steps too,
                that soft ground sometimes treacherous beneath our feet,
                and a broken ankle here could be viper deadly;
and my nose cleansed by the water taking it all in,
    all the different odors, smells, and scents,
        including a rotting carcass here and there twitching my face.

When Widow took his turn on the lead
   my mind tended to wander some,
   my just following easy in his tracks,
      sipping water through the camelback spout
      and responding instantly to his signals,
      as he had mine on lead;
and I thought about our conversation that last night,
   which in turn reminded me of another conversation,
   the very night before we took plane for Paraguay.

That conversation was one with Rez and some others,
   and Mosetta there too, 'Soul Sista' we called her,
      kinda mocking Bill Clinton, I suppose, our beloved Prez,
   and her worried some about us and giving us her support,
      (and I suspected even then she had secret love for Widow);
and there in the mess hall we sat having coffee late,
and Rez the resident Christian conscience in our unit,
   (every unit has one),
and a good man was Rez, been through a lot,
and his call sign always brought us a smile,
   especially Mosetta, always damn near laughing to hear it,
   but truly not in any demeaning way.

Like married couples shooters and their spotters,
   at least among the Harlot Moor's,
we are always referred to by both our call signs,
   first shooter then spotter.

For us, it was Frisco and Widow,
   for Frisco Drifter and Widowmaker,
and then there was Khan and Boomer,
   and also Diego and Banshee,
      (the Moors the only unit with women frontline,
      and how Colonel Mooring got away with that,
         well, your guess as good as mine,
         but still were no female shooters),
   and Black and Blue, another team,
      originally Black and Bloom,
      but comm talk changes things.

And then there was Death and Resurrection,
   and quite a story that led to those codenames,
   a hugely disrupting turmoil throughout the entire unit for a time,

  although obviously it had its comical side,
finally forcing Colonel Mooring to step in and fix it,
  using his personal power to do so,
  (and let me tell you that fixed it quick),
and that's an interesting story I'll get to in due course—
  no, I think I'll tell it now.

Rez

Actually Rez originally wanted Death and the Preacherman,
  which if allowed would have been it, end of story,
but Brass vetoed that like they did Frisco Drifter for me,
  until they found out I was born in Santa Rosa.
Sounds silly I grant you, but it had some logic in my case
  the logic being my codename could never be traced to me,
  jihadists with long memories and far reach, even into our records,
  my identity possibly revealed simply by matching up our birthplaces.

In the Marines these things are important to Brass,
  giving them vindication for their lofty status,
  thinking up and nodding to bullshit like that,
    or so I thought at the time.

So Rez made it Death and the Razor's Edge,
  simply because he liked that film,
and his voice preaching often compared to a velvet razor,
  and don't ask me how that got started,
  every one saying his voice cuts right through you,
    but oh so softly, so very, very softly.

But because of phonetics,
  (like Black and Bloom to Black and Blue),
Razor's Edge first became 'Razor's Action'
  whether spoken over comm or personally in the Unit,
and hearing that you might think the next step easy,
  everyone evolving to saying 'Resurrection,'
but o-o-oh no-o-o-o, came a giant step in between
  that if not for Colonel Mooring stepping in
  would have knocked Rez right out of the Marines.

Came out of the French Quarter in New Orleans,
  the closest city to the Unit's Headquarters and training,
from one of those porno stores there in the Quarter,

graphic posters right in the windows,
and found there apparently by someone from the Unit on leave,
    male or female never determined,
    from the dollar rack of badly made videos,
came an old, old video with Rez' youthful face on the front cover,
    a graphic porno, and no mistaking his baby face,
and that video circulated through our Unit like the Asian flu.

Turns out he made it when he was 17,
    and already well into drugs, especially cocaine,
and the title was <u>Man with a Lance,</u>
    and starts with Rez in some silly black leather armor
    riding on a horse to some captured queen,
        (the first and only time it turns out
        that Rez ever rode on a horse),
and every woman in the Unit watching it in private,
    (and passed around quickly as I said),
every woman confessed they gasped like that captured queen,
    first time he drops his knightly tunic.

Quickly, as in just about overnight,
    and this I only know from hearsay,
when his call sign got spoken,
    first on comm and quickly amongst personnel,
it went from Razor Action to Death and Razor's Erection—
    very funny, many yuck's those 2 on a mission,
    or behind his back in mess or elsewhere.

Beyond embarrassing was that for Rez becoming such a hot item
    and it forced him to go public to everyone,
telling everyone in groups the circumstances of it,
    him deep into drugs and in need of money
    when that video was made, at 17.

But that was not enough,
    that nickname just so phonetically ingrained,
just so easy to say, an easy snicker to boot for payoff,
and it got to the point of Rez trying to quit the Corps,
    knowing that nickname would follow him everywhere,
    even though now known for his Christian faith—
        and not as a thumper, not at all,
        but a sincere guy just trying to be a Christian,
            for him the way out of both the drug life

and the porno world to which he had fallen prey—
Rez way more like the publican in the temple in silent repentance
than the fat Pharisee prancing and boasting his Jehovah blessings.

That's when Colonel Mooring stepped in for him,
    for a stout-hearted man, so to speak,
and he had all of us except Death and Rez,
    (their then out on a mission),
had all the rest of us gathered together,
    the entire unit then there in New Orleans,
    snipers, scopers, comm, and support staff,
        quite a number of them women of course,
        but none immune to "Razor's Erection;"
and Colonel Mooring had us all stand and laugh,
    his saying it himself in his stentorian voice,
    "Razor's Erection," and ordered us to laugh,
the Colonel just flat out ordering it walking center aisle,
    repeating it again and again as he did,
and that went on for at least a minute, us laughing on order,
    if not even a bit longer,
and then he stopped and snapped at all of us in anger:

> "Shut up and sit down. That's it. That's your last laugh ever on that. Next one laughing goes on report. You do not hobble a good man for a mistake he overcame big time, resurrecting his life back up as he has done…like few men have ever been able to do…out of drugs and lowlife and made himself not only into a Marine to be admired but a man to be respected no matter who or wherever he is."

> *(Colonel Mooring looked over us all,*
> *his walking that center aisle. He was steamed.*
> *He knew he was right but even more important*
> *we knew it too. But he also knew the power*
> *of language, and that also needed to be addressed.)*

"For that reason, his call sign is now changed," said the Colonel, almost a sneer at us. "Now he's Resurrection. It's Death and Resurrection. That's what it's gonna be. See if you can live up to that."

Colonel Mooring was not religious either,
   no more than a passing familiarity with Christianity,
but he respected those for whom it was a revelation,
   a steppingstone to an inspiring and trusted camaraderie,
as surely it had been for Rez.

It just fits in this case, he said of that call sign,
   and us a small Unit, he could get away with that.

Rez, as you might guess, was surprised and delighted,
   and honored too when told of this gathering while they were gone,
   and especially honored because he admired Colonel Mooring,
      more than any of us I think, even me,
and indeed this was like a medal to honor a triumph in his life—
   Death and Resurrection, which for him shortly became Rez,
and all the rest forgot, only that triumph remembered,
   like wounds long healed but the Purple Heart forever.

Of course much of it was because he was so good at his job,
   not only as spotter but also keeping Death under control,
   the 2 of them as a team equal to me and Widow,
      the two best shooting teams in the Unit,
   and that is not something a commander wants to lose,
      especially if so because of some youthful misstep or prodigality,
         (prodigality not the word Colonel Mooring used).

Colonel Mooring subsequently ferreted out that video
   and handed it to Rez to personally chuck into a garbage fire.
Never was a man prouder, and the ultimate upshot of it all
   was what Rez became for all of us,
   for men and women both throughout the unit,
a trusted confidant, and especially the confidant for Death.

Every unit in the Marines,
   probably every branch of the armed services,
has its resident Christian blowhard,
   and every unit its wise old sage;
and ours was the only one I ever heard of
   whose both were the same guy,
though blowhard was never a word for Rez,
   and what his real name was I don't remember.

Just suffice it to say that Resurrection is Rez,
    and Death a shooter from a different planet,
and him and me the best in the Unit,
    and fortunately Rez able to hold him in check,
    the only reason Mooring would accept their codenames,
        someone to keep the straitjacket on Death,
        (and Widow saying, see it's always the black man,
        always the black man has to deal with Death),
because if truth be told Death *was* our best shooter,
he just never missed, whether target or man,
    but a different planet, I tell you,
    and so said everyone.

And here's another truth to be told—
    even though the Moors not a big Unit,
I never met him for one reason or another,
    Rez, yes, a number of times,
    but Death never, not even once.

It just happened mysteriously, vagaries of the Marines,
    that wherever I was, he was not,
    something akin to Clark Kent and Superman.
But the odds were so long against it that after a while
    I just assumed he was avoiding me on purpose,
        (like I said from a different planet).

Yet 3 times in my life did Death save my life shooting,
    one time with a shot totally amazing,
        a miracle really.
Still, though in the same unit, we somehow never met.

His true name was Stossel, that one I knew,
    but no one ever called him that.
Death was he always in our Unit,
    from the day I arrived, a cherry-breaker,
    until the day I left, something else entirely,
and his icon a black gloved hand,
    and in that hand a silver bullet,
        (truly must be from Pluto, I thought
        my own icon being the Golden Gate Bridge),
and always Death— no other moniker ever used for him.

Anyway that night before Paraguay we were talking,
   all of us having coffee in the mess hall,
     and Death on leave to his home appropriately named,
        some Midwest hick town called Hawkeye, Iowa,
and I was sticking it a bit to Rez and his religiosity,
   right after he mentioned something about God,
but he was patient with us, me and Widow both freaky that night,
and no doubt because of my personal angst I said:

> "Look at what we do, Rez. How does that reconcile with God. Are we the good guys here?"

> "Look around you," said Rez. "We all die. Is this something to die for or not, and your comrades too?"

>> *(I just shrugged it off, not yes, not no.)*

> "Where there's evil there will be blood," he said, "and always it takes blood to answer blood. Christ answered blood with his own blood. And so must we if it comes to that. We have to not only be prepared for that but willing— not volunteering like Christ maybe, but willing."

> "Willing," exclaimed Widow, full of the same angst. "Willing! Tell that to Death when you see him. I don't think *he's* willing. The other side *is* willing, those Jihadies, way beyond willing. They're flat out excited to jump on a bus strapped to a bomb. What do you call *that*, Rez?"

> "I call it evil," said Rez.

>> *(He seemed more than a bit offended our even asking, and I saw Mosetta really perk up at his words.)*

> "Evil is always the *other* guy," she said, anticipating Widow.

> "I'll tell you why it's evil and we're not," Rez retorted.

>> *(Widow sniffed at the air like someone had farted.)*

> "I think I'm smelling some bullshit in the air," he said to needle Rez.

"This is not boolshit," Rez responded with some offense, yet remained patient. "I'm not telling you nothing I don't really think's the truth. If it ain't it's cause I'm just not capable of seeing it. But this is no *bool*shit. Saying that means you don't know me. Are you ready to listen to what I got to say?"

(Widow was sipping his coffee and just nodded,
two sugars, two creams,
and I always kidded him not taking it black.
I could smell oranges out of the blue.)

"My bad, go ahead," Widow said after a moment's reflection, he and Mosetta too sitting back for this.

"They're killing innocents and know it," said Rez pointing at Widow. "They delight in it and are using the killing of innocents to cause fear. Terrorism. You ever heard of that?"

(Widow just shrugged,
and with some disdain.)

"Come on, Rez," he said, "Master of the Obvious."

(Those were my words from before
and Widow had loved them,
Master of the Obvious.)

"You do that," Rez responded instantly, "you willingly attack the innocent and you just screw your cause, and whatever you stand for becomes completely worthless and meaningless… beyond worthless… to the point of atrocity and you gotta be stopped, no matter what. That was the lesson of Nuremberg, and if the U.N. had any guts at all they'd proclaim it all around the world. It's gotta be stopped."

"They're afraid themselves of a bomb up their short hairs," I said.

(That made Mosetta laugh, almost a spit take of coffee,
and I got a good kick out of seeing that.)

"It doesn't matter," said Rez. "Where there is evil there will be blood. And only blood stops blood."

"Good to know," I said. "That's certainly cheery."

"That's just us being the stick," said Rez.

(Rez was referring to the 4 rules of International Diplomacy, at least according to the Harlot Moors—
1. *Loudly trumpet your carrots and sticks.*
2. *No sticks then soon no carrots.*
3. *Get sticks.*
4. *Moors are sticks.*

"What about Hiroshima," demanded Widow. "And Nagasaki too?"

(Widow was demanding some answers, and not really demeaning Rez.)

"That's a tough one, no doubt about it," said Rez with a huge sigh. "That's as tough as they come. Who's the good guys there?"

"I'm listening," said Widow, his eyes intent on Rez, "and don't say strategy here. We're talking stuff way beyond strategy. You're a Christian, Rez, so how do you reconcile Hiroshima with God?"

Widow had him all right, and Rez was reeling some,
   but instead of flinching or shrugging it away
Rez reached right down to his soul for an answer,
   and you could see he felt Widow deserved it.
Given our agenda next day in Paraguay,
   he no doubt felt absolutely Widow deserved his best,
and Rez was going to give it to him.
Agree or not you gotta love him.

"All I can say is when you don't rebel against evil, then it's *you* become evil," he said without hesitation, "and even your children pay for it too, if you don't recognize it, that snake in the grass evil, and that means you can't protect them from it either, and they get bit as hard as you."

"That sure sounds real just," said Widow.

"That's a hard one sure, children stuck to the fate of their parents. Still, the Japanese people all knew the horrors of Manchuria and the Philippines, and China and Korea too, what their soldiers had done and were doing. They all celebrated the invasions and those victories, and also the brutality of those occupations. All of that has consequence, parents *and* their children. Yes, absolutely it's hard to accept, let alone understand."

"Come on," said Widow, "don't bail out on me now. Aren't you the one, Rez, banging the Christian drum. Come on. Give me a straight answer here or just shut the fuck up."

"Look what Vietnam did to us as a nation," retorted Rez, a bit put off but patient, "the people rising up against it ferociously."

"A bunch of sniveling long-haired twerps," I said with distorted face, a mock of right wingers.

"No, Stevie," said Rez, "it was conscience and the consciousness of a moral atrocity. The Japanese did not respond to theirs, nor the Germans either, and it cost them their nation in a horror way beyond imagination and they'll never *ever* be the same again, not ever. Vietnam cost us too, big time, just not nearly as much because we responded morally. Where there is evil there will be blood, and that horror did not happen to us the same way as it did to them, nor did it to those in the war who *did* abandon evil and fled it from Germany, to England, or wherever, or come to America."

"Just like Sodom and Gomorrah," I said like some catechism kid.

"Exactly," he said.

"Don't look back," said Mosetta.

> *(That made only me laugh,*
> *no one else getting it except Rez,*
> *Mosetta and me nodding at each other.)*

"Apparently not," said Rez. "It's like after the war. No German would ever admit being a Nazi."

"And no American admitting he was for Vietnam," said Widow. "*Now* it's become a point of honor."

"You got that right," I said. "Look at Clinton prancing and jiving and then wrapping himself in his antiwar stance like a Ghillie suit."

(We all at the table laughed and shook our heads, imagining the prez in a Ghillie suit.)

"You're saying our rebellion against Vietnam saved us," said Widow.

"At least for a time," said Rez, "a revival of our moral fiber, and there are always sniveling twerps, Stevie, whenever the people rise up."

"You got that right," I said. "Half the Sons of Liberty were street thugs and twerps, just swept along with the others."

"Murderers too," noted Mosetta, "there in the Continental Army."

"When the people rise up," said Rez, "they bring their diseases with them along with their inspiration. You got to look at things clearly, or at least try to."

(He sipped at his coffee and a bite of a donut.)

"Where there is evil there is blood," I repeated.

(Mosetta nodded, my obviously taking the words right out of her mouth.)

"Always," said Rez, some donut in his mouth, "and you gotta separate out the innocent or die trying. That comes with the job. Doing that separates you from the evil. You can see the Colonel understands that completely."

"How can you even say that," said Widow. "He's no thumper."

"No, he's not," said Rez, "not even religious I don't think, and he's a Nam guy too, as we all know."

"Then how can you fucking say that?"

"Look at this Unit's mantra," exclaimed Rez exasperated. "Must be blood, must be player, must save life. All of those must be met or you just don't pull the trigger, no matter what. That's the mind of Mooring, right from his own lips. Don't you get it. He learned from his experience in Nam. He understands it, the morality of it. That's what it takes to be the good guys."

*(We all nodded and for the time being Widow accepted it,
Rez's thought, perhaps not one of total clarity,
but certainly one deserved more pondering.)*

"I'll get back to you on that," Widow had said.

"*Do* that," said Rez, with total sincerity.

Destination

Like I said, the trek was easy enough through the bush,
   opportunity for double time opening up often,
   and therefore absolutely no problem with schedule.

One time we stopped for a breather, an open space in the bush,
   a bit of a valley and our stepping over a very narrow creek,
and we just splashed our faces without drinking from it,
   and that after taking a leak and finding it fascinating,
   our urine draining in opposite directions on the ground.

Then we knelt on one knee facing each other, the Harlot-Moor way,
   Widow saying it's a black-white thing, obviously, the opposite draining,
and me saying O, stop, that's just a myth, counterclockwise,
   Widow saying don't you believe your own eyes,
and me saying science says it's not the truth,
   one hemisphere to the other makes no difference,
then Widow saying, black-white, I'm telling you,
   seen it with my own eyes,
and me saying, nothing as blind as your own eyes.

We had heard many bird sounds in the bush during our trek,
   some like chalk on a blackboard,
but there on one knee we heard one just delightful to the ear,
   a long series of warbles and trills, pleasingly melodic.

"I wonder what that is," said Widow.

"Oh that's a tufted titmouse," said I.

"A tufted titmouse, you say."

"Oh yeah, they're a common pet in San Francisco, just about everybody has one. You can hear 'em out the windows when you're just walking down the street."

"I got your tufted titmouse right here."

(Suddenly we heard it again from a different direction,
obviously a response, but slightly varied,
a love story, pure and simple.)

"Look at that," I said, "two high branch lovers and you a vulgar varmint if ever there was one. Now don't you feel ashamed."

"I got your shame."

"Break's over, you vulgar varmint. Let's go."

"I got your vulgar varmint."

"You know it was kind of pretty, those birds," I said, leading out.

"More than a little," said Widow behind me.

The Target

This old Nazi lived out in the middle of nowhere,
   and apparently in his last days was running low on money,
      obvious to us because his security was minimal and cheap,
         only 3 guys to watch his back, said Intel,
            (we'd only see 2),
        and a kennel of dogs of course, maybe 6 or 8,
            (turns out now only 4).

He had a nurse and a housekeeper-cook,
    his house on acreage requiring a 4 wheeler for access,
    a very rough looking road leading west to civilization.
Once he had had a 6 man security team and 6 or 8 domestics,
    but obviously now was he falling on hard times,
the last of his money apparently getting eked out carefully
    by some department of Old Nazi Welfare.

The Intel was very specific and very detailed,
    including several photos of the people and grounds,
telling me and Widow this info coming from one of them,
    a domestic likely, probably the nurse:
        the informant adamant that old Nazi a short timer,
        and also where he'd be each afternoon.

The only true challenge was a near 200 yard crawl,
    after we donned again Ghillie suits for camouflage,
a crawl down a slope through tall greenish-yellow grass,
    then unseen we'd go along an arroyo
    leading us to the south side of the house,
and up on its crest to our shooting perch,
    us using drag bags all that way just for certainty,
    even though his security seemed incompetent.

There were no outposts we were told,
    and no booby-traps to worry about—
        Intel which proved dead right on.
But what else would you expect from security,
    near 50 years of nothing happening,
    no assault, no one coming near,
total and complete isolation and security boredom,
    truly them like lookouts for dangerous glaciers.

And that crawl was done totally in afternoon sun,
    our sucking on the spouts of the camelbacks,
    the water tasting harsh now of chlorine,
and down that slope we had gone on our bellies slowly,
    gently pushing fingers through that greenish grass, drag bags behind us,
    the chances soaring of our disturbing some snakes,
    and therefore our total alert for Tommy Goff,
        or any others of his deadly kin,
but coming down slowly, taking an hour
    any snake felt us coming just slithered away.

Basically we knew with this guy's security team so lame
    that all we had to do was not stand up waving and shouting,
    or flipping them off both hands overhead;
but truly the only thing was our not exposing metal to the sun,
    our not causing glint at them from the slope—
our only possible blunder to set them in motion.

Other than that it was really easy,
    and though not yet on perch we were an hour early on target,
our then crawling beneath that crest to the south side of the house,
our perch to be there because of his afternoon habit,
and we had already stopped beneath the crest
to assemble my M-40, old Kooshmensadah,
    one of my 2 names for it that just made Widow shake his head,
    this one coming from the book The Journal of Taranis the Helvetian,
        the name for that great red bow of Taranis,
            Death-Comes-Like-The-Wind.
My other name for it when I was in comic mode
    was my Vorpal-40, to honor Jabberwocky.

Over the top, Widow had said about those names, way over the top,
    how about Schizoid, he said, did you ever think of that,
and don't tell anybody else those names or it's Section 8.

I just smiled because those names pleased me,
    especially in training my first few times handling it,
an instrument of death and I knew I'd be good with it,
    and I just needed something to give it another face;
but Widow would never use either name,
    and he himself referred to it as my 'Thunderstick.'

When it comes to a weapon of death,
    everybody just needs their own personal magic about it.

The Rhododendron

We had not yet really seen his house, working our way to the south side,
    and then our crawl up from arroyo to the crest,
and us told by Intel to be on the alert for his rhododendron,
    for it would tell us we were absolutely in the right place,
    a true specimen they said, none like it in Paraguay,
    on the south side protected from the sun.

Keep your eye peeled for that rhododendron, I wise-cracked to Widow,
    when me and him started up from the arroyo to the crest.
A specimen, said Widow, we better get our scopes ready,
    and maybe take a cutting or two for those assholes at Intel.

You can't miss it, Intel had told us, and that tells you it's him,
    and their tone was coy, their withholding something,
and we almost thought they'd break out giggling telling us.

A rhododendron, we said, you mean a flower bush,
    and me and Widow just looked at each other.
Oh yes, they said, it'll catch your eye for sure,
    A specimen, they said, none other like it in Paraguay,
    probably not even in all South America;
yet truth be told, we were totally unprepared for it.

When they called it a specimen they had not done it justice,
    like calling the Pacific a body of water.

Peeping over the crest to the south side of the house,
    no big villa this or anything ritzy at all,
    just a large rustic 2-story made of local woods,
        dog pens to the east, and an old barn and garage.
        Two Australian 4-wheeler Range Rovers out front,
and what I expected to see was a colorful rhododendron,
    maybe waist high, maybe several together,
    possibly even several sharing a trunk,
something like the rhododendron garden in Golden Gate Park
    but instead what we saw was truly spectacular.

Massive in size, taller than his two-story house,
    not pear-shaped but more like a minaret,
    not as big as the main minaret at Taj Mahal
        but bigger than either of the 2 beside it,
        only not so pointed at the top.

A *huge* impact of color it was on our eyes,
    even at 100 yards as we were,
    and of course a lot closer in our scopes
like a sudden flood of color coming right at you
    and bowling you over before you can even move.

This was a huge tree and in full flower,
    a number of separate trunks entwined at its core,
        each a foot to 18 inches thick.

In color think dazzling neon pinks but mostly intense scarlet reds,
    though some clean green and white gave it highlights,
and all spread as if finger painted on a huge easel,
    and those bright red and pink flowers just seemed scalloped in texture,
and so suddenly seen its effect eye popping to us,
and circling its base a huge round carpet of mostly pink blossoms,
    as if the tree had just dripped a bright pink
    carpet of dew circling around it on the ground.

Think Jackson Pollack, what he dreamed of doing with color,
    something to stun and stagger and marvel miraculously,
and growing this huge rhododendron old Jack of walked away satisfied,
    and never faced another canvas again the rest of his life,
just gone ahead pell-mell and drunk himself to death a lot quicker.

I know I'm going on about this tree,
but it was a sudden huge wave of color upon us
    not only through my scope but the naked eye too,
    and not just to the eye but piercing right to your spirit—
        more impact by far than the Rockefeller Christmas tree,
            even with its bright neon lights on for skaters —
I mean this rhododendron just took your breath away.

        "*That*," said Widow, "is the most beautiful tree I've ever seen in my life."

        "Ya think! It's unbelievable," I said. "It's like he painted it totally with the brightest of acrylics."

We both took eyes from our scopes and looked at each other,
    our painted green and black striped faces,
    his more green, mine more black with his lines on me,
and then we both knelt back on our haunches,
taking breaths as one does after seeing the spectacular,
    as I had done in Spain 5 years before,
        up close and personal to Picasso's Guernica,
            but absolutely diametrically this the opposite experience.

"That tree has *got* to be 40 years old," I said, "6 trunks I think."

"I counted eight," said Widow, "foot to a foot-and-a-half thick."

"My God," I said, "this guy spent the last 40 years of his life making that…tree, this old *Nazi*. Remember his bio?"

"Yeah, brutal was the kindest word."

"How can this be?" I said. "How can that old Nazi, this Vlad the Impaler, grow this tree, Widow. I'm telling you absolutely, this the most beautiful tree I've ever seen, *ever* in my life."

"You got that right, Stevie. Me too."

"I always thought red mimosas were the most beautiful, but this rhododendron tree just dwarfs them."

(Widow just looked at me, shrugged, and blew a sigh,
 nothing really more to say, a total mystery.)

"Fucking A," I said again, "do you think this tree'll make any difference when he meets his Maker?"

"This asshole," said Widow, "hell no, not a chance. He might as well do stand-up at the Pearly Gates."

That's cracked us both up equally behind the crest,
    just one of those things,
especially Widow having no belief in an afterlife,
and we had both pulled back from the crest,
    choking down our laughter,
just the thought of it,
    this old Nazi face-to-face with the Almighty
    saying, "Hey, God, take my wife… please,"
        and then doing a soft shoe to boot.

That had my chest hurting from guffaws,
    me pounding my gloved right hand on my M-40 stock,
    and then as well on the grass and dirt.

For the moment the entire mission—
    spirit, plan, and execution,
the whole thing had come to a crashing halt,
    our laughing and howling like that,
halted like a plane hitting the side of a mountain.

Killing the Old Nazi

    "That tree is going to get in our way," I say.

    (We are calmed down now, looking back over the crest,
        first looking and then our creating the shot,
       both actions together bringing reality back to us,
      like some giant jellyfish settling down upon us.)

    "We got to find the perfect trajectory," I say, "and I'm assuming he's gonna sit in that wicker chair there on the porch. Can't shoot through the tree. Gonna have to shoot under it."

Me and Widow move around some,
    not using conn just our voices whispering,
us practicing several different setups,
    and do so until we find the right one,
but no wind and 100 yards only,
    I can do this one half liquored up, no problem,
    maybe even falling down drunk,
and any failure by me means failure of heart,
    some conflict of spirit or nerves conflicting my aim.

Right on time, in fact 10 minutes early,
    and out he comes for his afternoon constitutional,
    his nurse leading him, the 2 guards beside him,
        and where the 3rd guard's gone,
           errand, vacation, termination, or siesta,
    we don't know and we don't care.

Yet all these things together confirm it—
    the nurse bringing him out early,
    his leaning heavily on his cane,
their sitting him in that huge wicker chair facing south,
then her wrapping a multi-colored blanket around him,
    making him stand out like a Robin Hood target,

and the 3rd guard missing,
   likely sent on a wild goose errand,
not to mention all the detailed Intel we had,
   even to the point of this crest to shoot from—
all that totally confirms her to me as the informant,
and money or Justice who's to say what's driving her,
   maybe she's getting blackmailed by the Mossad,
   maybe she just cannot stand to see him suffer,
   or maybe she just wants a better job,
      and therefore has given him up to the Israelis,
      and her résumé all typed up and ready—
any or all of that maybe possible.

In my scope I can see his face,
   and him a wizened old geezer indeed,
the kind of white-haired old man people make jokes about,
— "I'm telling everybody"—
and they settle him down into the chair,
   the nurse and guards helping him sit down to his fate,
   her of an age and kindly face that could be his daughter,
and she definitely is tender and gentle with him,
   far more so than the 2 guards helping her sit him down
   into that large wicker chair with huge back there on the porch;
and no doubt in my mind what this is for him,
   and every afternoon through his final days,
a beloved rendezvous with that gorgeous rhododendron,
   like a grandfather come out to see his grandson cavort.

Then all 3 of the others go off into the house,
   leaving him alone with the tree and his thoughts,
maybe the nurse to the kitchen for coffee and strudel,
   to sit there wondering if this be the day.

Out of the side of the house within seconds both guards go,
   carrying buckets on the way to the dog pens,
obviously this be feeding time,
   the dogs bustling about in the pens, anticipating and drooling,
and I wait the shot to use their howling as sound cover,
   and that happens quickly, the guards pitching them raw meat,
which of course will make these dogs well fed,
   should it come to pass their pursuing us.

"I see only 4 dogs left," whispers Widow, using his spotter scope. "This old Nazi's definitely going bust. I can handle those four all by myself, me and the Fox."

(The Fox, as in Silver Fox, Widow's ivory-handled 9-Mike pistol, which had won him twice the pistol marksmanship trophy.)

"Whenever you're ready," Widow whispers, looking up from his scope and over at me. "No wind, no significant elevation, and short distance, we could throw darts at this guy."

(The dogs were now really howling.)

"Just put the crosshairs on his heart, Stevie. It's a can't-miss shot, center mass."

"Look at that guy, Widow, look at his face."

(The Nazi's eyes are open, looking our way, almost as if he can see us.)

"This guy's done awful things," I say, "I mean he even strangled children. Can you see that, Widow? Can you see that on his face?"

"No, he's just another old fart, but he's the guy, no doubt about it. That's the guy, Stevie, the old Nazi for sure."

"What do you think coming down to the end of his life? Do you think he's sorry?"

"It don't matter, Stevie. He could be pissing his pants sorry. It just don't matter. You can't do what this guy's done and put a hand to your heart and say hey my bad, how about a replay. Sorry, man, Colonel Mooring's right. You kill the innocent, especially you kill children, and you're never not a player."

(No doubt Widow's having 2 daughters makes it resonate even deeper in him than me.)

"Look at his eyes blinking," I say.

"Do it or don't, Stevie, but fucking make up your mind."

With my teeth I pull the glove off my right hand,
   the taste now of thick leather in my mouth,
and suddenly the smell of oranges in my nose.

      "Can you smell the oranges, Widow?"

      "No," he says like I am crazy.

         (Widow is the only one in the Marines knows
         I've had all my life olfactory hallucinations,
         especially coming when I get excited.)

My bare hand takes position now,
   after one last adjustment to the scope,
   right index curling around the trigger,
and as happens every time I am ready to shoot to kill,
   a huge calming like hush comes over me,
hard to describe and it creates absolute focus,
   like the dark cloths that old time photographers
   threw over their heads to close off the world,
   —Matthew Brady shooting bodies, blue and gray,
      scattered and piled on Civil War battlefields,
truly that kind of focus and calm,
my eye in the scope for the killing.

      "I just wish 'Evil' were written on his forehead," I say.

      "Oh sure, and how about 'Easy Lay' back in high school."

      "Never make a shooter laugh."

      "*Now*, Stevie. Who you gonna be?"

      "Guten Tag, you fucking Nazi."

The dogs are more barking now then howling,
   not nearly as loud as they had been just before.
Crosshairs over his heart directly,
   trajectory barely under the bottom limb of that rhododendron,
I squeeze the trigger ever so gently,
   and am almost stunned when my M-40 fires.

When a round goes by your ear you hear it loudly,
   the sound barrier crack and whoosh of it truly harrowing,
     (as I would learn in Iraq in time to come),
but struck center mass, like this old Nazi—
   you never hear it coming.

In less than a second of time,
   one second from decision to execution,
that M-40 round rockets 2 inches under the rhododendron limb,
   the sound wave of it breaking loose several leaves,
then strikes his chest and severs his heart,
   only a bit of a yelp on his face,
   something similar to getting ass struck by a hypo,
just enough time in his mind to realize and know
   he is being killed by his fellow man,
   and to know exactly why we are killing him.

Then off into the void he goes,
   him face-to-face with the Almighty,
and all that terror inflicted on innocent souls
   does *he* now know 10,000 fold,
and all of that happens before the leaves dislodged by the bullet
   flit and float gently down upon the blossom pink ground
   circling the gathered trunks of his beloved rhododendron.

In that second my realizing the sum of all this,
   I actually feel sorry for this old Nazi,
   but no regret, not even an instant,
     absolutely none at all for killing him.
What goes around comes around—
   Justice is served;
yet a human soul so drained and twisted by all that Nazi evil,
   as absolutely by the records this man has been,
that in itself is truly a horror to behold.

       "Perfect shot," says Widow, a very professional voice. "He knew.
       You could just see it in his face. He *knew.*"

         (A moment of silence fell as we continued
         to look at him through our scopes.
         Then Widow pulled back first.)

"Now let's get outta here," he says. "It'll be an hour maybe two before they even realize he's dead. Let's go do our thing there at the creek and then on to the river and across it."

"Do you feel any different? Remember, we're a team. It's not just me."

(Widow pauses for a moment to consider.)

"No," he says, a bit of surprise in his voice.

"Me neither," I say, "not a bit, just like I had shot a mad dog out in the streets of some cracker southern town."

"Yeah," says Widow, pointing a finger at me, "exactly like that. Let's hope they're all like that. I sure could get used to that."

(Turning from the old Nazi he slaps me on the shoulder, pleased with our business.)

"When we get back to the river, Widow," I say, "remind me to tell you about a guy named Walter Jürgens."

"Who he?"

"A Nazi."

"One fucking Nazi's enough for one day," he says. "Let's roll."

"You mean let's crawl," I say.

"Yeah, Warp Speed," says Widow.

Aftermath

Funny for a while after killing him,
   one thing we both did do was become more garrulous,
far more than before the shot.

To move faster through the tall grass this time,
   and to jump up if spotted and hightail it over the crest,

we did not use drag bags crawling up slope through the grass,
   just backpacked it in our Ghillie suits, M-40 slung over my shoulder,
   ready for use if needed against those security guards.
But crawling quickly like that, "warp speed,"
   that caused us two encounters we could have done without.

The first was our disturbing a nest of black beetles,
   and out they came racing over us and our packs.

      "What the fuck," groaned Widow, speaking for me as well.

Frustrated like me was he, but maintain we did our discipline,
   and quickly but gently began brushing and sweeping them off,
first from our necks then those running up our faces,
   spitting those reaching near our mouths,
   and snorting those hurrying into our noses,
     and they did have an ugly smell, even a foul taste,
and Widow's nose way bigger than mine
   made for a more inviting beetle spelunking,
     therefore me more spitting
     and him more snorting.
Thus we repelled them with minimal movement,
   and continued our crawl.

      "They're like coffee beans sprung some legs," said Widow
      snorting

     *(I reached out my hand, gloved again now, and brushed
   some of the beggars off his neck and from under his floppy,
     him doing the same for me and from my pack.)*

     "These are fucking black hive beetles," I said.

     "So?"

     "Books says only in Africa to worry about them."

     "That's right, and the States too, old Loosiana."

     "They shouldn't even be here," I said.

"Then they're some Re-animator's cup of morning brew broke out and running for their lives."

(He flicked one off trying to burrow under his glove. They really did look like coffee beans.)

"A Re-animator you say. Maybe these Nazis really were into black magic evil."

"Oh stop with black magic," said Widow, "before you go and get yourself into trouble."

"Black on magic evil isn't the same as black on people."

"Oh now you gotta stop."

"Just like white on people isn't the same as white on rice or white on pus."

"Are you hearing what you're saying?"

"It's just connotation," I said.

(By then we had crawled well beyond the beetles.)

"There's no connotation on racism," he said. "It's like… dark night coming down."

"There you see, you almost said it yourself, black night coming down."

"I'm gonna come down on you in a moment."

"No you won't."

"Why the fuck not?"

"Because you know I'm right."

"Yeah, right up your skinny ass with my boot, that's what's right."

"So you're threatening violence on me. Tell me again, who's the racist?"

"There's no end to you."

I had more to say, and ready to go toe to toe,
    if one can do that while sniper crawling,
but that was the moment of our second encounter,
    and unlike the beetles, totally unlike,
this was an encounter of a deadly kind.

Now finally did we come face to face with snakes,
    not one but two, and 6-footers at least,
    big tropical rattlers and they were mating,
us just bursting into their boudoir.

One took off immediately, hightailing it behind us,
    but not the other— it was rattling pissed,
and rose up like an S above that grass,
    now rattling even more madly— truly damn scary—
    about to strike at my face, my M-40 awkward on my shoulder;
but Widow pounded the grass hard beside me,
    using his fist to draw its attention
    as he snatched his Ka-bar out of his belt,
and turned it did that snake and struck at Widow,
    his blocking it deftly with the flat of the blade.

The damn thing was quick and still grisly rattling,
    and rose up and struck at Widow again,
    but this time *I* was ready, shed of my rifle.
A snake in the grass strikes with projectile speed,
    and its mouth wide open like the trunk of a car,
    if the trunk lid had two venom-dripping fangs.

I stuck out my gloved hand and snatched it by reflex,
    just catching its striking head in my right hand
    like a shortstop snatching a liner going by,
        something as shortstop I had done many times;
then with a twist of the gloved hand to lock it in,
    I just gripped its head in my hand to hold shut its jaws.

The thing thrashed and shook to break itself free,
    trying its best to wrap its 6-foot-plus self around my arm,
and a powerful struggle for me to hold it in grip.

Really remarkable it was that viper-serpent,
    its face now in total darkness and fighting for its life,
    its length much longer than me on the ground,

all of it twisting and thrashing so violently
    that my hand seemed throwing punches at Widow.

Finally down I forced it on the dirt at base of the tall grass,
    Widow seizing the deadly thrashing serpent next to my hand,
then a flash of the ka-bar and Widow's leaning hard on it,
    the soft ground not making it easy,
but then after a crunch and spout of blood
    its head came free in palm of my glove;
and also remarkably its severed body thrashed a bit,
    like a lid rattling on a countertop,
before in an instant it gave up the ghost,
    flopping down lifeless upon the grass.

Me and Widow looked at each other, panting heavily,
    me afraid to even open my hand,
and both of us quickly looking around for the other snake,
    but it was long, long gone, so to speak.

Down I slammed that ugly snake head base of the grass,
    and watched its jaw open slowly by reflex.

        "Male or female," said Widow now, regular voice.

        "Oh that was the bull for sure," I said, "and boy was he pissed."

        (At same instant both of us looked back at the old Nazi,
        dead and upright in his afternoon perch, still totally alone.)

        "You know," said Widow, "I'd like to take that head with us."

        "Snake or old Nazi?"

        "The snake, you ding dong, but I don't want poison things like those fangs anywhere on my person."

        "Nor in *my* drag bag either," I said.

        "At least with beetles it ain't curtains for sure."

        "Ya think?" I said.

        "Let's get going. Sayonara, asshole."

"Oh, you mean him," I said. "For a moment there I thought you meant me, given what we were talking about before."

"*What* were we talking about before?"

"It'll keep."

>*(Back again we looked at the house,*
>*the 2 security guards still at the dog pens.)*

"What a couple of humps," snorted Widow.

"Lucky for us," I said.

"He'll be there in that chair until supper gong."

"It's not like anyone really cares about him, except maybe that tree."

"You got that right," said Widow. "Probably these guys won't come looking for us even when they find him. Probably more concerned where their next paycheck's coming from. So why would they even chase us now?"

"We can't count on that."

"Bet you, Stevie, they bury the guy and say he died of cancer."

"You think the Mossad will let them get away with that?"

"Probably not," he laughed. "But it doesn't matter to us now."

"I still don't feel a thing about killing this guy," I said. "Do you?"

>*(Widow shook his head.)*

"No more than killing this rattler or exterminating rats."

>*(We both looked each other in the eyes,*
>*our faces painted green and black,*
>*and truly we both realized our sincerity.)*

"Who you gonna be?" we both said in perfect unison, bumping our fists.

"It's not going to bother me none either," said Widow, "us getting the hell out of snakey Paraguay."

"Yeah, let's hope our next mission's in Ireland."

"Ireland, yeah," said Widow cheerfully, "there must be some Old Sod Nazi Jihadies need killing there."

"Oh, Laddy, please don't you be putting a cap up my ass," I said in my best Irish brogue learned from Sean Coughlin.

(That made Widow smile and even laugh a little.)

"Gotta take the good with the bad," he said.

"Let's went," I said.

That last was actually a bit of homage to an old TV western rerun,
   one I loved as a kid, the Cisco Kid and Pancho,
   the only one of those old westerns in color,
and so loyal to Cisco was old Pancho,
   ready to die for him if need be;
but unlike Cisco he struggled with English,
and he was played by a great old Castilian Spanish actor,
   a guy named Leo Carrillo, veteran of many movies,
   but 70 years old and just playing out the string
      in this cheap TV western show made in the 50s
      and me seeing them 20 years later on re-runs,
         long after Old Leo had his face-to-face with the Almighty.

Yet as a kid I liked him way more than Cisco,
   and something about him just seemed tragic,
   his last days pretty much playing the buffoon;
but no buffoon in real life was Leo Carrillo,
   a great state conservationist and a huge influence
   in getting Hearst Castle to the people of California,
      and made available for anyone to tour and marvel at,
and yet his having to play out the string like that,
   well, it just gives me grief.

And I can tell you he would have loved that rhododendron,
   which itself as an isolated specimen like it is
   cannot be said to be part of real life ever for anybody else,
     exactly as Hearst's Castle was before Leo Carrillo,
but then again maybe it is now because here I am
   remembering that tree and talking about it,
and remembering as well Ol' Leo,
   a better memory for me than that fucking old Nazi;
yet that old Nazi loved and was loved by that tree.

Life sometimes does seem such an infinity of mirrors.

The Last of Rhoda

Laying atop of the grassy slope we looked back for the last time,
   some for security but mostly a last look at Rhoda,
each of us through our different scopes.

> "You know the only thing concerns me," I said, "is who will tend it now?"
>
> "That thought crossed my mind too actually," said Widow, looking at it through his scope, "but it's a sturdy thing and after 40 years it's got to stand on its own."
>
> "And who's gonna love it like he did?"
>
> "It's a tree," said Widow exasperated. "What's it gonna feel?"
>
> "Look at it," I said, "how beautiful it is, the only one like it in all of Paraguay. I will never forget that tree, and you won't either, most beautiful tree I've ever seen or maybe will *ever* see."
>
> "Yeah, that's probably true," said Widow. "But what's your point? He just watered it and tended it. Everything else comes out of the tree."
>
> "Don't you think that beauty is a response to love, not another like it maybe in all South America. *His* love."

"Nazi love, what a concept."

(Widow just shrugged and raised green eyebrows.)

"Anyway nothing we can do about it now," he said, "collateral damage."

"Yeah you got that right," I said, "collateral damage, the loneliness of Rhoda, now and forever."

"You're killing me here, Frisco. You want me boo-hooing that damn tree. Those guards may be humps but there definitely not paralyzed."

"Nor their dogs either," I said.

"I don't know about you," he said, "but I could use a bath."

(Looking again at me he took a sniff.)

"Second thought you could too," he said. "Did you shit your pants back there or something?"

"That's just your breath blowing back in your face," I said. "Let's went."

The Getaway

The crest of the slope was now finally at our backs,
   packs adjusted on our shoulders,
   my M-40 broken down in its canvas bag,
   9-Mike's and ka–bars both at ready,
and those Ghillies quickly folded and stowed.

Normally we would have cast aside those Ghillies,
   their bulkiness hell on speed and quickness,
but by orders no trace or imprint of us to be left behind,
   nothing to connect this killing to the USA,
and thus our not even to bury them.

After a quick leak taken to not stop on the trek,
    and absolutely no concern now about being seen,
we double timed it west to that creek,
    figuring two hours before dark, three at most,
and though unlikely our being pursued,
    we executed our escape plan strategy at the creek,
    a strategy planned before we had left on this mission.

        "We probably don't need to do this," said Widow.

        "Safe than sorry," I said, and he nodded.

Because good trackers always chase you upstream first,
    we sloshed that way but only 50 yards or so,
then exited on the west bank and double timed it,
    making a large loop together through the bush,
    ending of course back at the creek.

The purpose was to occupy and confuse them for a time,
    both the trackers and the dogs,
their probably crossing back over to the creek's east side,
    and then wasting time chasing upstream some more.

But actually back into that creek and south we sloshed
and about half a klik downstream found what we wanted,
    a huge tree limb out over the creek and within our reach.

Up on it we pulled ourselves and our gear,
    cautious of snakes for sure out on the limb,
        our not needing any more of that,
especially those Tommy Goffs so had my attention,
    even though none supposedly here this far south,
        (the book was absolutely certain of that,
        but it was also certain no black hive beetles either),
and if not Tommy Goffs to worry about
    then always of course its dangerous kin,
        especially red striped corals sunbathing on limbs.

Over that huge limb we both crawled to the massive trunk,
   just about 10 feet from the green-covered creek bank,
then shinnied down, no sound or sign of anyone following,
   our throwing some powder lye we had brought with us in a tin,
   both on the tree trunk and behind us to kill our scent,
turning west and double timing when possible through the bush,
   Widow on lead handling the compass,
although unlikely they'd even pursue us,
   and even more unlikely catch us if they did,
   especially with dark night falling heavy on us soon.

After a single klik we took a needed breather in that heat,
   heads thrown back, sweating heavily,
our hands on our thighs, breathing hard.

No way they'd chase us into this belly of menace, I agreed,
   not for a man already dead, and only four dogs.
Remember, Widow said again, you get what you pay for,
   and what a couple of humps.

Not the first time his saying that,
   once before back on the crest,
but this time it burst me into laughter.

      "Who's the humps, them or us?" I said laughing.

      (That made him laugh too.)

      "Point taken," he shrugged. "Let's skedaddle."

      "A couple of humps," I repeated, securing my floppy tight and laughing, "you're killing me here."

      *(I don't know why it didn't seem so funny
   that first time he had said it back on the crest.)*

Back to the fast-moving river, much of it double time we went,
   stopping on a low crest for a look back and seeing nothing,
me then saying if you want a bath let's stumble on purpose,
   us not being cherry-breakers anymore.

Widow smiled and nodded affirmative,
   and turning west off we went again double time,
   and for some reason it seemed a lot easier trek back to the river,
     our land-nav easy, and that mount northwest now an easy marker,
and nothing at all behind us to be concerned about.

Crossing Over to Campground

Once again we crossed the river before nightfall,
   so as not to cross it first thing in the morning,
and as well by the book keeping it as barrier.

Holding our gear and Ghillies overhead in the waters,
   we both indeed pretended to stumble,
ducking ourselves down, faces and floppies under,
   the water so cool on salty skin,
   black and white, safe and confident.

We even stripped naked reaching the bank and back in again,
   the water after first blush feeling delightful,
    our washing any filth off our assholes and crotches,
     absolutely not urinating in the water,
   and after checking each other for leeches and tics,
     both of which of course harder to spot on Widow,
   even washing the camouflage paint off our faces,
    the soft touch of our bare hands now feeling the stubble on our cheeks,
     and on our bare skin too without clothes or camelbacks of course,
   yet keeping an ear out for hounds just in case,
     and an eye out for snakes there in the fast moving waters.
Then emerge we did from that brisk no return river,
   both of us as naked and clean as new born babes,
my sense of smell washed and cleansed,
   had enabled me to smell the fresh water itself.

The sun was hot enough even late in the day
   to dry us and our field cammies both,
     in spite of the humidity,
and we just squatted on the bank eating our last MRE's,
   in fresh socks and boots and drab underwear only,
    the skeeters and bugs and critters not yet out in force,
     (but our 9-Mike's within our reach for snakes),
and though MRE's they still tasted delicious,
   heated by those chemical packs they carry,

mine chicken and his steak and so we shared,
> me dipping my spoon into his pouch for some tasty steak
and his into mine for some definitely saucy chicken,
> something like a fondue pot supper in the jungle,
even scraping those pouches with bread for every last drop,
> neither of us able to get enough,
>> *(though we did save the energy bars for the morning).*

> "You know, thinking about it, Stevie," said Widow, us eating from each other's pouch, "you probably saved my life snatching that snake the way you did."

> "Yeah, you're probably right, no question."

> "Hey, where's you being humble, telling me I saved yours?"

> "A sniper with humility?"

> "Yeah, what am I thinking!"

> "Tears of a sniper," I said.

> "Yeah, yeah, more valuable than the Medal of Honor."

> "We always said rarer."

> "Yeah, well I got the steak. You got the chicken."

> "Hey," I joshed, "you saying something about my courage?"

>> *(I actually could feel the silence fall,*
>> *and looked up from my MRE pouch,*
>> *his eyes dead set on mine.)*

> "Never, Frisco. I would *never* say that about you. Not ever."

>> *(That was the most appreciated compliment*
>> *ever I had gotten in my life up till then,*
>> *and absolutely the most cherished.*
>> *I just smiled, not beamed, just smiled,*
>> *and nodded my thank-you to Widow.)*

"Better eat that last piece of steak," I said. "It's gonna be a long ride
until our next meal."

By training habit we kept that alert ear to the east,
   a habit which, as we both kidded ourselves,
     would likely be with us for the rest of our lives,
our scrutinizing everything we ever see and hear;
and us doing all that of course after reporting the kill,
   Widow sending the new code I created just for this mission—
     "Tommy Goff, Tommy Goff, Chilo down. I repeat,
     Chilo down... Chilo down…Tommy Goff out…"

Not Comrades Now but Brothers Talking

This time it's me off to the edge of the bush and back,
   pants down in a dangerous scene and vulnerable posture,
and always a very private experience dealing with your own shit,
but truly another world when squatted, pants down to your ankles,
   on the edge of the jungle, hearing deadly things big and small,
and your 9-Mike gripped solid in both hands your squatted there, safety off.

Returning to our site I understood Widow's enthusiasm the night before,
   my totally escaping with my life from pure vulnerability,
   my leaving our MRE trash buried in the same hole with what it creates,
and me now grinning like Michelangelo or da Vinci.

Back I come imitating Widow's ghetto voice.

> "Ooo-eee, jim, I just had me a noble shit, and ooo-eee am I now brave and magnificent."

> *(That did make him throw back his head and laugh.)*

> "And now you wanna delve into things profound," he said.

> "Ooo-eee, jim, you've been reading my mail."

No fire set and really none needed,
   another wall of rocks for our heads curved like a shrine,
     the netting in place like a ski slope over our bodies,
and we lay covered in our night wraps and Ghillie capes,
   and remained silent for a time face-to-face.

Us on the opposite bank that night it felt so immensely different,
    even though that river still ran gurgling head to toe.
Suddenly Widow spoke up, the Harlot Moor whisper,
    and that's another habit you just don't break.

> "That's interesting, Stevie, even profound, what you said about water."
>
> "You mean the presence of Infinitude"
>
> "Yeah, exactly."
>
> > *(That pleased me profoundly his liking that.)*
>
> "How so?" I said.
>
> "If water is like you say, how Infinitude enters its presence into our reality, us slaking it in to inspire and enthuse, as you said so eloquently, then drugs are demons entering us differently, maybe something like getting fucked in the ass."
>
> "Jesus, Widow!" I exclaimed, "where'd *that* come from? And demons! I can't believe *you* said that…*de*mons."
>
> "Just thinking."
>
> "Hey, maybe you're right," I said. "Maybe that's why AIDS seems beyond disease to human atrocity. Demons where the sun don't shine. It sure gets people's attention. What a horror for them."
>
> "Don't get me started on that," said Widow.
>
> > *(Like the bulk of the black community
> > Widow was no fan of the gay agenda.)*
>
> "Still," he said, "drugs are the Axis of Evil."
>
> "Is that access or axis," I said. "Be clear."
>
> > *(Obviously he wanted to talk,
> > and I was trying to encourage him.)*

"*You* know what I mean."

"How does it work then, Widow, tell me that, how that Axis of Evil comes and demonizes us."

"Fun and frolic, that's the one side of drugs," he said, "hyping the nervous system beyond all normal experience, beyond the design of Evolution."

"Evolution has no design," I corrected. "It's effect without cause, or any plan at all… or so they tell us, and saying different is total heresy."

"Whatever…then hyping beyond the confines of Evolution."

"I get it— neurological stim and pleasure of a non-Sapiens kind, including hallucination, sensitivity, and reality beyond all normal human capability, impossible under natural neurologic condition and function. Therefore, it is experience that requires corruption, especially of the synapse and dendrite, not to mention corruption of neurotransmitter activity, perhaps even the axon itself, totally beyond all system design, causing the false experience of altered states."

*(I shut up, thinking I had impressed him enough
with all that blarney and waited for his reaction to that.)*

"Okay, Einstein, I'm impressed. You've had way more science than me.. I give it to you, Stevie."

"Just clarifying," I said.

*(He liked it when I sometimes strutted
and punked him like that.)*

"Corruption is the word describes it best," said Widow, "just like gangsters *and* their politicians."

"And certain priests," I said.

"Yeah, them too."

"And on the other side?"

(Widow took a long breath here, and that's when I began realizing he wasn't just bird-turding about the horror of drugs.)

"On the other side," he said, "lies debilitating addiction and that includes corruption of the mind, not only beast ugly but psychotic as well."

"You mean neurologic rebellion and tyranny causing annihilation of insight and clarity."

*(He was giving me disdain now—
I couldn't see it so much
as feel it in the dark.)*

"Something like that," he said.

"A Marxist revolution in the CNS itself, the proletariat axons and Dendrites throwing off frontal lobe and Betz cell tyranny, seizing total control of the hypothalamus and corpus callosum and even the brainstem itself, not to mention the pituitary too, taking control of all neurologic manufacturing and transportation and even the hormonal centers of learning *and* adaptation."

"O, s-t-o-o-o-p," said Widow, "you're killing me here. Who's telling this story, and besides it's more like Animal Farm, except it ain't funny."

Immediately by his tone now I understood,
   and totally fell silent,
   no more joshing or needling.
This was personal, no doubt about it,
   not only personal but as deep as it gets,
a profundity he now felt ready to reveal.

Widow then went on something of a rant,
   totally unusual for him
   and alerting me even more—
this was personal.

"If you've seen people addicted, Stevie," he began, "when you've seen what I mean, seen the asshole of humanity, seen the ugliest life has to offer, worse than ugly, worse than murder, worse than rape or savagery or even beating someone fucking senseless. You seeing a human being cut off totally from whatever spirit truly makes him human, that's a unique horror."

(That got my attention, his saying spirit.)

"You mean cut off from Infinitude," I said.

*(I gritted my teeth.
I just couldn't help saying that.)*

He just nodded his head in the dark,
    thankfully disregarding my needle,
something obviously now rising up within him,
    something brought on by our cherry-breaking trek,
and I just shut up totally my jabber now and listened,
    and in so doing got the truth of Widow,
and yes indeed the truth will always set you free.

Widow Talk

Someone cut off from spirit like that, he said,
    (his actually using again the word 'spirit')
they become a demon, virtually by definition,
    not a zombie or vampire, none of that shit,
but truly a living demon.

He's no longer your son or brother,
    (Widow's not adding 'sister' or 'daughter',
        a Mosetta feminist courtesy we accepted,
    told me absolutely this was personal
        and had to do with brothers.)
Expect no mercy from him, said Widow,
    expect no humanity either, not a drop,
but expect instead a nervous system locked in rage,
    from brain to fingertips and every stop along the way,
someone totally cut off from their source,
    whatever Infinitude is, if it is,
and him totally acting on instincts,
    but instincts set on fire and screaming—

no rationality, don't even try, totally berserk,
   only the barest remembrance of humanity even available,
   and pretty soon not even that, totally gone.

That's the curse drugs bring, he said,
   some worse than others I grant you,
   way, way more violent some,
but all of them cutting you off from your soul,
   the only way to describe it, he said,
and that's soul like black people say it,
   cutting you off from the source of your being,
from that Infinitude, he guessed.

Those that make those drugs, he said, those who sell them,
   and even give them away to hook you,
those who put them in the hands of children,
   kids with systems not even fully matured,
those are the ones truly Monsters from the Id,
   (a phrase he liked that I had taught him),
the demons and gargoyles skulking on the streets.

      (He actually said, "stalking," but I think he meant "skulking."
               Then he fell silent for a few moments.)

   "Tell me how you really feel," I said.

            (He chuckled a bit hearing me say that,
            my saying it giving him a chance to choose—
            whether stopping now or continuing on,
            whichever, I was willing to listen sincerely.)

A way deep breath and sigh he took,
   the kind people do before letting it all out,
baring their own soul of horror seen and deeds done.

> "Just even *wit*nessing that process, Stevie, human experience turning into a total self-inflicted nightmare…and not just yourself but the people who love you…just watching that over a couple of years, someone you love demonizing their own soul and then de*vour*ing it in a kind of ruthless cannibalism…just watching that you are never the same, just not ever the same… like a kid seeing a real battle and actually seeing somebody's head get blown off in front of him. You never get over that."

Widow now told me of his brother,
   one of a set of twins 5 years older,
     (Jeremiah— named for his mother's father,
     Matthias— named for his father's father),
and Jeremiah the brother Widow idolized,
   even more than Matthias,
never a problem telling them apart,
   even when he was 2 or 3 years old.

Handsome and athletic was Jeremiah, basketball and piano,
   a kid that was truly loved by everyone,
     especially those of the female persuasion,
yet he got himself addicted, thinking he was superman.

That horrified Widow because he so loved Jeremiah,
   who not so slowly turned opposite now to his twin Matthias,
which turning also horrified Matthias,
   both of them having grown up one mind, virtually inseparable,
     having each other's back at all times,
     their then protecting Widow and his sister,
       and woe to anyone molesting either,
     a personal security for the two of them priceless,
but Jeremiah's addiction in the course of time
   brought the two twins to each other's throat.

Early in college for Jeremiah had come cocaine and speed,
   and never the same after that,
   a growing horror witnessed day by day;
and Widow blamed Matthias at first and then their dad,
   his beloved older brother more and more deceitful and angry,
   and more and more violent and in the end dangerous to them all,
until finally they had to throw him out of their lives,
   totally and virtually like a rabid dog,
   none of their fault, only his,
his far too long having robbed them and threatened them,
   and even harmed each of them physically on occasion,
     and that included his mom and dad,
to the point that only legal consequence prevented Matthias
   from shooting Jeremiah the Demon dead in cold blood.

That's when the family finally came together in grief,
   turning their backs completely on the once beloved,

no contact at all, not even taking messages,
    always hanging up the phone when he called.
It was like City gates closing and locked,
    and Jeremiah out beyond the walls—
and one year then slipped to another,
    and then another and another.

Came one day then the tragic coincidence—
    Widow in New York City for a football game,
        (wide receiver for the Northwestern Wildcats
        he was, which had been Jeremiah's dream),
and he gets a call in the locker room from Matthias,
    a message intercepted meant for their parents,
    a message sent by the New York police.

After the game, accompanied by his coach who insisted,
    down to the morgue goes Widow, fear in his heart,
and there he is, Jeremiah, dead in a drawer,
    throat cut and tortured face,
    his body found in a Bronx alley, discarded,
his reign of violence and malevolence ended by a straight razor,
    and the detectives quite willing to tell Widow all about it.

All of that throws your own soul on a rack,
    or so said Widow in the dark, the river gurgling,
    and insects buzzing and striking our netting,
and lucky for him that coach had insisted,
    Widow totally a mess immediately,
    and nearly flipping out their long flight home—
a grief for which he had no prep or experience,
    but fortunate he was for his coaches and teammates.

Not only are you not the same after that, he said,
    but no way to get back to being anywhere near the same,
now totally cut off from whatever was your lifeline,
    (and that's the word he used— 'lifeline').

That next week he dropped out of college,
    straight downtown Chicago and joined the Marines,
        his parents upset of course his doing so, mostly his mother,
            (as were mine, and especially my mother),
    but his father mostly understood, *(as did mine),*
        even angrier than Widow with Jeremiah,
        as you might expect a father to be.

In the Marines, unlike me, Widow's one goal only and certain,
   to become a scout sniper and learn those skills;
and then after 2 hitches to retire and join drug enforcement,
   applying a sniper's skills to bring those bastards down.

Truly unlike me Widow had his lifeline laid out before him,
   how it would go and what it would do,
      (although his wife and 2 twin daughters were a bit of an audible,
      necessitating a third and last tour in the Marines.)

Still, he had existential purpose for his being,
   and more than anything I admired him for that,
certainly more than the size of his dick,
   him and Kahn vying comically over that primacy,
   but neither to their credit letting it get beyond comedy.

Drug addiction, said Widow that night by the river,
   is such a terrifying reversal of the Cinderella story,
   turning snakes and vermin into human beings,
their then peddling and marketing wicked dreams and concoctions
   to ensnare not only Dark Nighters,
   but the naïve and callow as well,
all of them thinking those drugs taking them to some exciting ball,
   but instead it ends in Whitechapel whoring, and Jack the Ripper;
and each of those peddling snakes eventually pipe dreaming
of whacking their way up to a cartel Prince of Darkness,
   wealth and power like Kubla Kahn,
   and a stately pleasure dome of amazing delights,
   where Alph the Crackhead River runs
      on down to a sunless sea.
Oh yeah, like that's gonna happen.

And so pursued Jeremiah that dream with a savage vigor,
thinking he could dominate an underworld of Evil,
   huge violence that in the end turned on him,
   like gaping jaws driven by hunger and greed.
His once beloved brother turning in the end violently evil,
   that's what devastated Widow that long flight home from New York.

The agony of it, said Widow, the agony of addiction,
   it makes even a casual observer shriek in terror,
to have a fellow human being seize your hand painfully,
   begging you for relief to set him on fire.

"And there was Jeremiah trying to become one of them, not only addicted but one of those snakes, Jeremiah, who I loved with all my heart, gonna bring those drugs to our people."

"That's rough," I said. "It does not *get* much rougher than that."

"Hell it don't," he exclaimed.

>*(His voice rose way above whisper before he caught himself and returned to discipline.)*

"You wanna know what's rough. I'll tell you what's rough, what really devastated me on that plane ride home and got me joining the Marines. You really wanna know?"

"If you want me to."

"Then I'll tell you, Stevie. I was glad he was dead. That's the truth, I was glad. Matthias was right. We should have shot him dead like a mad dog, and what really kicks my ass is I wished I had done it myself, maybe not cut his throat but put a round right through his heart, just like we did that old fucking Nazi."

>*(Some huge bug hit our netting and Widow smacked it away with the side of his gloved fist, and there for a moment I actually thought he'd grab his 9-Mike and shoot the thing.)*

"That thing in the drawer at that morgue had no connection, none at all, none to the Jeremiah I knew. Like Old Yeller we should have put him down. Saved us a lot of grief, and a lot of lives too."

>*(He took a breath and a long sigh again.)*

"He killed a lot of people, Stevie. I never told my parents, and I didn't even tell Mathias. Just kept it to myself. He killed a lot of people and was gonna bring that horror to our kids."

>*(A few moments of silence passed again.)*

"The horror of it, Stevie. It was just the absolute embodiment of human horror."

"You might get some run for your money on that one, I said."

*(Mostly I was just trying
to soothe his aching spirit.)*

"I'm talking individual," he said, "not A-bomb or Nazi horror. My own brother, fucking Jerimiah, was one time a bottom feeder like that old Nazi and each had himself an appointment with ancient excrement."

*(He took a last a deep sigh,
a signal of finality.)*

"Let's get some sleep," he said. "We got a bit of a jaunt tomorrow and those assholes won't wait."

Those last words, "ancient excrement," I never understood,
   and I don't think he meant me to,
nor did I pursue it, Widow played out emotionally,
and me with no remedy for him but silent comrade,
   a role the Monsignor had laid out for me and Sean,
   that Sunday morning mass so many years before,
laid out like a golden threadbare chasuble,
   the one he wore that day for mass
   that needed Rose Bauman's needlework attention,
after he had sat all night with her dying father.

"You're right," I said, "let's get some sleep. Just be alert for snakes… I mean the Tommy Goff kind."

"Forget about them," he snapped. "Books says not this far south."

(A moment's silence in that absolute jungle darkness.)

"Widow?"

"Yeah." Very faint.

"I'd have killed him too, if he were my brother."

"That's why I told you.

Returning to Civilization

Next morning we were up, virtually same instant,
   and were washing our faces, squatting at the river,
   after eating our energy bar saved from the MRE,
     and this after urinating both of us into the river,
     absolutely defying the parasite myth,
   and Widow saying he hoped we're not pissing on the Infinitude,
     me saying he's probably used to it by now,
   and look, it's all swirling clockwise anyway, same as home.

Then suddenly when we stooped to slap water on our faces,
   there it was, there in the river coming and going,
   a huge snake an arm's reach out in the water in front of us,
     absolutely longer than either of us,
     just getting itself carried along to its fate.

        "Look," I shouted, spitting some water. "I told you. Tell me that's not a Tommy Goff."

        "I'll be damned," said Widow, jerking his hands back. "It just might be."

        "Oh yeah, the book," I said. "You can always count on the book."

            (We watched the snake carried out of sight,
              and I swear it truly was a Tommy Goff.)

        "Let's paint and get rolling," said Widow. "That Huey won't wait. *That* you can count on. I doubt those army guys will even get out to take themselves a leak, afraid of that parasite up their dicks even in the grass."

To save time we stood and painted each other,
   him more green, and me more black,
him saying, wait you missed a spot,
   and dabbed lines down my nose and across my brow,
   really setting that superstition for us;
and off we went through the bush,
   double timing it whenever we could,
   mostly running in tandem, sharing the point,
     my quick reflexes making him feel safe;

and neither of us that morning, not even once,
    even mentioned that old Nazi;
but we did mention that rhododendron tree,
    Widow saying he even had a dream about it,
and I said it must've been in color for sure,
    and he said, yeah, yeah you got that right,
    a colored man with a colored dream,
me saying I can't believe you even said that,
    and him saying that's just one between you and me.

Per orders, like we had done that entire trek,
    we attempted no further radio contact,
and we just waited on the edge of the rendezvous clearing,
    squatting in the bush under some trees,
        totally pissed off, us way early and then them 15 minutes late,
            very unprofessional outside a war zone being so late,
and neither me nor Widow any doubt of our position.

> "Fucking GI's," said Widow, "we should never work with them."

> "We had to have them this mission. We needed them for urgency."

> "Even so," he said. "Put your Ghillie on Stevie."

> "Why? They said we didn't have to coming home, just painted faces."

> "Just do it. Humor me."

We both did so and waited squatting ensconced in the bush,
    and finally we heard it coming, then overhead that Huey plenty loud,
    our not talking without shouting from that moment on,
and their circling and hovering knee high above the clearing,
for a three-minute wait only, the copilot looking at his watch,
    the same two who had dropped us off the morning before.

Us in our Ghillie suits at the tree line,
    facing them right straight in front of the Huey,
    facing right at them, a stone's throw away,
and still they could not make us out squatting there just inside the bush,
and they waited uneasy, looking at their watches, checking clipboards,
    way obvious that the jungle made them fearful.

When I started to stand from my squat,
    Widow seized my arm quickly and firmly, holding me down,
and his gloved hand signal insisted we wait 2 full minutes more,
    the Huey hovering loudly, the pilots more and more freaky,
        looking in all directions totally on edge,
          like a Great White would jump up under them and seize them,
            or maybe those parasites leaping on their legs through a window,
        but still they just could not see us in our Ghillies.

Then on his tap we rose together and trotted out slowly,
    Widow leading the way,
    and each of us taking a grip up from the guy in the Huey,
        the Asian Oriental copilot who then shouted out,
          "Cutting it close, aren't you?"
and we just nodded and said nothing at all,
    totally anonymous in our Ghillie suits,
and just sat securely, our backs against hard metal again,
    our drag bags now under our knees,
        my M-40, Kooshmensadah, broken down,
          and safely stored beside me in its canvass case,
an occasional drip of hydraulic fluid on our gloved hands.

Later, after debriefing and our after-action report,
    I asked Widow why he had done that,
us just squatting there while they hovered and waited.

> "First," he said, "was to pay those motherfucking army guys back for being late on a mission. They were sure nervous, weren't they, those assholes, just hovering above the jungle, not even standing in it."

> "And the second?"

> "To show ourselves and them we were *going* somewhere and not just fleeing the bush in fear of our lives. Who you gonna be?"

> *(I smiled at that and banged his fist.)*

> "I thought you'd like that."

> "One for the good guys," I said

[The End]

Excerpt from HighPockets:

The Whore of Babylon

Now am I going to pick up again with Scarlett,
    and this time from the very beginning,
she who often called herself Woman of the Night,
    but that was her mostly in comic mood,
yet sometimes when caught up in the bleak and melancholy
    would she then call herself the Whore of Babylon,
    and really at those times nothing I could say or do,
just wait for the walls of that Bleak House finally to collapse.

$1000 a night is where the bidding began for Scarlett,
    and not just for her beauty alone sought and paid for,
but also her abundance of charm and wit on somebody's arm,
    to impress CEO's and other upper management types,
or anyone else could use and afford her bright mind,
    plus of course that rare beauty and elegance of hers,
Scarlett even creating soirées sorting with elegance and charm
    the complex human currents of business and commerce.

And not always, she told me, her assignations a sexual encounter,
    especially for gay men and academic or boner-less intelligentsia,
    and them in dire need of a female companion to be impressive,
but only them with the money of course, always the money,
    to satisfy whatever their needs and prideful desires.

Yet were also there those in her life of an evil kind,
    one of whom truly who came to shudder our souls,
    and him I'll get to in due course,
but whether that evil kind a karmic consequence of her profession,
    like Jezebel the wife of Ahab subsequently devoured by dogs,
or whether just an outrageous misfortune like Anne Frank,
    a beautiful soul in a tsunami of malevolence—
that I cannot say.
You'll have to make up your own mind on that one of course,
    and that after you get all my absolutely biased take on Scarlett.

Still that grand a night was also to pay Scarlett's expenses,
    (or so she told those few who questioned),
expenses like a secret bodyguard, someone close by stealthily,

(as she always told clients, but never was one really,
just the threat of one always enough for her purposes,
not to mention the pistol in her purse and her a good shot);
and were expenses also totally of the beautiful kind,
    clothes, wigs, and make-up, and stunningly expensive shoes,
    (my eyes dazzled by her huge closet full of fine things),
not to mention limos and taxis and various drivers,
    her never driving her own Jag to assignations,
    nor even allowing clients knowledge of her penthouse,
    (and that a hard and fast rule never to be broken).

And all those expenses, I'm sure, right off her taxes,
    including that fore-mentioned 9-mike Beretta,
    kept as I learned in a drawer by her bed,
    (my not knowing that for several weeks),
and well-trained and well skilled was she with it,
    carrying it when needed special pocket in her purse,
and her well-practiced at extracting it quickly,
    the purse handles sliding along her left arm
    as she seized and pointed the Beretta both hands.

She showed me her move once to satisfy curiosity,
    snatching her Beretta out of her purse,
    (unloaded for that demonstration of course),
and really it was like a gunslinger's draw right out of the Old West,
my awhile calling her Big-Nosed Kate after that impressive demonstration,
    (not a nickname much to her liking).

Certainly was Scarlett world-class in those dangerous days,
    a match for Du Barry, Delilah, or Mata Hari,
and maybe even Pompadour, my eventual nickname for her,
    but used sparingly…very sparingly that nickname.

As beautiful as Quasimodo's Esmeralda was Scarlett,
    natural red hair, green eyes, and shapely figure.
Yet are there many women with a figure like hers,
    but few stand out with that hair and those eyes,
so easily picked out in theater crowd or busy art exhibit.

It is said you are only five phone calls from anyone alive,
    whether world-famous or in the outback of Australia,
    six at most depending on your influence;
and for me for Scarlett was it only one,

   my sister, who even made the call for me,
though *I* did not know it then at that time,
   that call drawing me into worldly intrigue,
a little something cooked up between the two of them,
   their hoping it something to benefit us both, me and Scarlett,
and their offering it to me one day over coffee at Dante's Inferno,
   HighPockets calling me there,
   someone special for me to meet—
that Scarlett intrigue destined to change my life,
   body and soul and all ways possible.

Meeting Scarlett

That was first time I met Scarlett, there that day at Dante's,
   joining them for coffee after their lunch,
my showing up sloppy— Levi's, pullover, and a Giants cap,
but her with that red hair pulled back by barrette,
   making those green eyes stand out beautifully,
   like night lanterns on the posts of a foggy wharf,
plus her wearing a beautiful hand-knit wool sweater,
   one with variable bright hues and colors, reds and blues,
   arranged horizontally those colors and accentuating her figure,
   (wool never wearable in summer except in San Francisco),
a sweater so standout visual it took huge courage just to wear it,
   no doubt turning all eyes on her entering Dante's,
overpowering my sister's dark beauty restrained by gray business suit,
   plus blue blouse and orange cravat of some fluff,
but her beauty no match at all that day for Scarlett's.

This was not a woman afraid to stand out, this Scarlett,
   and obviously not afraid of much else either in her domain,
and certainly was I more than a bit intimidated,
   and just listened at first to her quite delightful voice,
a voice with variable husky expression,
   kind of like her soft colorful sweater,
and therefore to me was it obviously trained, her voice,
   reminding me immediately of Mae West,
   from old movies watched, me and my mother,
and me now tongue-tied by Scarlett's beauty and presence,
   and both of them impatient with me too slow to follow their ruse,
   explained to me just before the coffee was served.

"You want me to take an acting class with Scarlett—"

"Studio," corrected HighPockets.

"— And me to pretend I'm her brother."

"Yes, exactly," said HP, "and it's only a few weeks, not even all summer, mostly, and you don't go back to college again until late August, so it works out perfectly."

"But I don't have any acting ambitions."

"Doesn't matter," said HP. "It'll be good for you."

> *(Scarlett's great eyes had been hard on me,*
> *and me struggling to maintain my poise.)*

"Why?"

Now two separate sensations happened simultaneously to me,
   two unrelated sensations causing a weird reaction within me.
The first was Scarlett now speaking up first time to me directly,
   and her voice absolutely thrilling, so Mae West husky and sexy;
and the second was suddenly in my nose the smell of coffee,
   the deep richly flavored Dante's Ethiopian kind,
though none of it yet delivered to our table,
   and it was like voice and smell were the same experience,
   like heads and tails on the same coin.
Very strange,
   especially to those who instead of napalm
   love the aroma of a good brew early in the morning.

> "Because acting is good for everyone's soul," said Scarlett, "no matter what it is you end up doing."

> "No, I mean why the ruse," I said.

> *(Suddenly was I able to gather myself out of intimidation,*
>   *a mysterious strength came out of nowhere,*
>   *a kind of instant blind trust in Scarlett,*
>   *though I know that sounds idiotic,*
>   *just there it was full blown.)*

"To be a shield for Scarlett," said HP. "Are you not listening?"

"You mean a Beard."

"Sort of," said Scarlett in that voice. She then smiled. "Actually, yes, a Beard… well put."

*(Now was I put to relaxed,
all my anxiety fading quickly.)*

"Finally, there you are," said HP looking close at me. "Now come on and get with the program here and tell us your thoughts."

"A Beard might not do it," I said, "not for young actors feeling their oats, with dreams of Newman and Brando and applause."

"Feeling their oats," said Scarlett, smiling at that.

"Young horses ready to run," I said with bravado and sweep of my hand.

(Although in truth I had only run once myself.)

"Feeling their oats," she repeated, a short laugh like a cough, then a nod.

(Obviously a phenomenon not unknown to her.)

"Why not a boyfriend?" I said.

"You're too young," said Scarlett like 'wake up dummy.'

*(I nodded and shrugged to that obvious reality—
my too young any way you looked at it,
her about the same age as HighPockets.)*

"Younger brother will work," said Scarlett.

Her tone carried a sophisticated confidence,
   which was lit up as well by her expressive face,
     and a gesture of hands very graceful,
certainly all of those qualities that any actress would need,
   not to mention her beauty spawning this Beard stratagem,
and now were we served cups of Dante's great Ethiopian coffee.

I would certainly do it of course, leaping on it gladly,
  something that promised a passage into real life and intrigue,
but still I did not want to seem too eager and obviously hooked,
and so drew my fingers slowly across the soft tablecloth,
  pretending to weigh the pros and cons,
then taking my first sip of that dark and rich Ethiopian brew.

"What's in it for me?" I finally said as if I cared.

"You want money," said HighPockets sitting back.

*(On her face was that practiced look of shock,
and one that brought from me a delightful smile,
her negotiating posture and ploy seen 1000 times.)*

"No, no, no," I said to her but looking at Scarlett. "You know for you I do it as a favor."

*(Now HP came forward darkly, elbows firmly on the table,
her breasts filling her blue blouse and behind
that fluffy orange cravat thing around her neck,
her leaning forward to close the deal.)*

"See it as kind of an adventure, Stevie," she said, "but totally without the dangers of jungle or sea of course."

"Going deep into the Heart of Darkness," I joshed her.

"Ooh yes," she responded, "but just as safe as mama's parlor."

*(The Heart of Darkness would turn out shockingly true,
and not at all so safe as mama's parlor.)*

Actually as HP spoke Scarlett was looking me over,
  her eyes hard into my eyes searching,
and if not for my one sexual relationship had in Mexico,
  though sadly doomed as it had been, adolescently tragic,
I might have looked away intimidated... but did not,
  and now she spoke directly to me,
  keeping her eyes locked on mine,
my last words hovering in her mind,
  what's in it for me?

"I'll think of something," said Scarlett, that sultry voice.

"Count me in in!" I said immediately.

*(She smiled now, that confident smile.
Of course she knew she had me
and at this point I didn't even care,
time on my hands and the prospect of adventure.)*

"You are a bit of an impetuous boy," she said.

"That's his middle name," said HighPockets.

"I'd pretty much do anything for my sister," I said, staying focused on Scarlett, so easy to do.

"Your eyes," she said now looking at both our faces, "the two of you, they're almost identical. I just noticed. I don't believe I've ever seen eyes like you guys before."

"They're Krayle eyes," said HP. "I'll leave Stevie to tell you the tale of that. I have to go."

(She had looked at her watch on her wrist,)

"Our grandfather was a notorious murderer," I said proudly.

"So it's agreed," said HP to me, picking up the check. "Just to be clear."

"Come on," I said, "you knew I'd do it from the moment you called me. This was just a screen test."

*(HP looked at me, raising her eyebrows with a smile,
letting me know she was pleased with me.
I in turn looked to Scarlett.)*

"Did I pass?"

*(Scarlett reached over and took
the check from HighPocket's fingers.)*

"You'll do," she said.

The Mystery of It

This acting class— studio— would prove to be fun,
    at least at first,
    and Scarlett after meeting me actually wanted me,
        that gave me an especially needed sense of worth,
as low as I had gotten after Mexico and Marlena,
        my first venture then into adult sexuality
and me laying an egg as big as Boston

Still, even though I could be occasionally precocious,
    mostly was I a callow and naïve 18-year-old,
and certainly very slow to realize how huge this gift from my sister.

Yet Scarlett had taken a liking for me almost immediately,
    an affection from first moment I opened my mouth,
or so she later told me huge smile on her face,
    and Mary a part of the mystery of it,
my having joined them for that coffee and not the full lunch
    because a college thing with Mary required me first,
        (a violin audition I accompanied her to at her request,
        me always able to calm her down before performance);
and for Scarlett my skipping a free lunch to help a friend,
that quickly added to whatever HP had told her of me,
    again something she later related to me,
and it even encouraged her to become a kind of guru to me,
guiding me through gender mysteries and the turmoil they bring —
    actually sorceress may be her better description,
    certainly more a mystical than magical version,
yet one who herself was not immune to dangerous powers.

But guide me she did and my good fortune,
    not only into sexuality and passion but romance too,
and the tender mercies men and women can have for each other,
    so many things about sex I had been bewildered by,
    or uninitiated into or stark raving blind to,
very much like some primitive mope living by superstition,
    not to mention half-truths and outrageous myths,
and it just pleased her in those weeks to tutor me.

What it takes many men a lifetime to learn, if ever,
    Scarlett taught me patiently in those summer weeks,
    and many other things, certainly some not by her intention;

and why she took that patience with me so diligently and effectively,
    far, far beyond my usefulness to her,
I never really knew, nor I suspect did she,
    ours one of those relationships way beyond understanding,
    like us taking over roles already developed by other actors.

But bottom line looking back and remembering,
    I was so embarrassingly naïve and sappy,
and how many times must she have rolled her eyes and sighed—
    well, they must of been legion.

**<u>Scarlett's Marvelous Penthouse,
the Views and the Music,
and Her Large and in Charge</u>**

My first attempts at acting in studio,
    which I'll get to in due course,
were at least energetic, if not Cary Grant suave and debonair,
    or swave and de-boner as the old punchline goes,
        a joke shockingly Scarlett had never heard, whose punchline
        quickly took on new life as a private joke between us,
        suave and de-boner.

My service as her "Beard" did become highly valued the whole time,
    especially critical beside her in that first week or two,
but always useful our whole time there in studio,
    a younger brother thwarting the pursuit of young lions,
including eventually the "Broadway" Prince conducting the studio,
    a theater actor named Gregor Obradovich,
him then a newly risen, ambitious, and touted young Broadway actor,
    now branching out to the West Coast his acting studio.

But like I find myself saying so often here—
    I'll get to all that shortly.

So callow was I with Scarlett at first, so sophomorically naïve,
    (and I can't believe how hard this is now to own up to),
but that afternoon Scarlett just took charge after coffee,
my not yet then understanding the cougar in women,
    that which relishes guiding young men into manhood,
her asking me to drive her home from Dante's,
instead of her taking a cab, a way for us to get acquainted—
    (I say this now with big smile on my face.)

Only 26 was she at that time, and so eye-popping beautiful,
    especially in that rainbow sweater she filled out so well
and quite a few heads turned to follow her out of the restaurant,
    and not just the eyes of men alone following her,
    but women too, whether lesbian or jealous;
but to me was she like a different generation,
    way more experienced and vitally knowledgeable,
like a blueblood lady to some poor vassal's son.

And home to her was an intimidating penthouse,
a many storied building standing at the top of Nob Hill itself,
    a front entry canopy reaching to the sidewalk, plus doormen too,
        one of whom always to open the door
        and the other always to run the elevator,
            (an old-fashioned Otis with rotating handle)
and that day was it Tommy running it,
    the one of them I grew to like the most,
and me introduced as her brother, and a little unsure of myself,
    especially that first time, the long ride up,
    me so wordless it's painful to admit to.

Because her carpets were newly cleaned, she said front door,
    she had us both kick off our shoes,
        (and me my socks as well of course),
and their placed orderly beneath the intercom by the door,
    upon which she flicked a switch,
music streaming immediately from a local FM station, KFOG,
    a beautiful sound filling her entire apartment, every room.

        "Great Bose speakers," she said, "two in each room."

        "Yes," I said, "I came across them big-time in high school. They can turn music into something you can almost touch and feel."

        "Exactly," she said, a bit surprised and glad I understood.

On my bare feet soft and delightful was the texture of that wool carpet,
    nothing like any carpet I ever trod before,
        (or should I say trode),
and the KFOG DJ announcing their continuing now with movie themes,
    nothing but movie themes all that afternoon.

Her apartment was of course luxurious and impressive,
   very fine furniture plus some interesting antiques,
but especially eye-popping were the floor to ceiling windows—
   there both in her dining room and living room,
   the north and east walls of her apartment,
     (which I would find included the east wall of her bedroom too),
astounding views dining room, from Golden gate Bridge to North Beach,
   then living room, downtown, Bay Bridge, and East Bay to San Leandro,
and on a clear day as far east as the Berkeley hills,
   (or so she told me, but not that summer day,
   a bit San Francisco gray and overcast,
   ergo her multi-colored wool sweater).

As I stepped closer to the living room windows for those views
came to my ears Laura's Theme from *Doctor Zhivago,*
   "Somewhere, my love, there will be songs to sing,"
those lovely violins and that plucked balalaika effect,
   a film thoroughly discussed back in my Art-App class,
   a massive film of the Russian Revolution gone wrong,
     (one of Mr. Walker's favorites of course, our teacher),
and it certainly put me into a certain mood now,
   Laura and Yuri and the ever menacing Strelnikov,
     (who one time had been Pasha, a pie-in-the-sky idealist,
     but then turned to the dark side Strelnikov, "The Shooter").

So astounded was I by those views and that theme,
   so lovely the violins somehow beatifying such stunning views,
my jaw just dropped… totally dropped to my chest,
Scarlett smiling and lifting it shut with her finger,
   the first time she ever touched me,
and became a game we played many times,
   me flabbergasted by one thing or another,
   and her finger just lifting my jaw shut,
     (a game me and Mary had played both ways since kids),
this time my seeing almost the entire Bay laid out before me.

        "How beautiful is that?" said Scarlett in her great Mae West voice.

        "As beautiful as you," I said without edit, absolutely spontaneous.

        (She smiled briefly, obviously accustomed to such,
           although of course never before from me.)

Look around, she told me, and help myself to anything,
    beer in the fridge if I like,
but forgive her she just had to take a bath,
    and we could talk through the bathroom door,
things to decide about the acting studio,
so grab a beer and go ahead and come on in,
    her pointing to her bedroom door,
    there in an alcove among several others,
and we'll just talk through her bathroom door.

Real Life Begins

When I did come through her bedroom door,
    a can of Coors in my hand half drained,
    more out of nervousness than any real thirst,
my hearing the bath water running full tilt
and the rhythmic 'Third Man' now plucked on a zither,
    the zither sound remarkably differentiated by that Bose,
        treble and bass as distinct as genders,
a film also seen and discussed in Art-App,
    Mary irritated with my take on it,
    my hoping the evil Harry line would escape;
but then was that cherished reverie suddenly dismissed,
    virtually swatted away,
first by the Bay again seen through huge windows,
    but then my suddenly realizing the visuals over her bed.

Not a mirror was it fastened there over her bed,
    nothing so common or gaudy as that,
        (not to say that can't be fun),
but instead excellent reproductions of world famous works,
    all set inside a cherry wood glass case,
    somehow solidly attached to the ceiling over her bed,
and though the works clearly of different kinds,
    her reproductions were all same size,
    and interchangeable at her whim,
4 of them each in its own compartment:
    Starry Night— van Gogh,
    The Persistence of Memory— Salvador Dali,
    From the Lake— Georgia O'Keefe.

The 4th was a scene from the Sistine Chapel,
   not God touching Adam into existence,
but the human form wrapped like a snake around a tree,
   on one side Eve prostrate before a naked Adam,
   like she was about to give him a blowjob,
which to gay Michelangelo may have only seemed appropriate,
   but then on the other side the two of them fleeing,
   fleeing in fear and sorrow, banished from Paradise.

All four as jaw-dropping as the views from her windows,
   outrageously beautiful reproductions overhead every night,
and all of them that moment did colorfully strike my eye,
   and for a time me unable to focus on anything else,
   even the Third Man theme fading away from my awareness,
a hell of a thing to wake up to in the morning light,
and me just standing there with contraband beer in one hand,
   (my being only 18 years old at the time),
totally struck by these magnificents overhead,
   three from long ago and the one way longer,
and now me pushing my own jaw closed freehand,
   and hearing the water turned off in the tub.
To say I was struck silent is to say God knows.

      "Oh dear," I heard her say, and the swish of her moving in the tub.

      (The door was only slightly ajar,
      and though I peeked I could see nothing of her.)

      "Are you out there, Stevie?" she called, needing little effort for her voice to carry, a good thing for an actress.

      "Yes, admiring your ceiling so beautiful."

      "Thank you," she said in elevated voice, echoing some there in the bathroom. "Listen, did I leave a purple bag on the bed?"

      "Yes."

      (I hadn't really noticed until that moment.)

      "It has my new soaps and shampoos in it. Could you possibly just reach it through the door for me?"

      "Sure," I said, again so naïve it hurts me now.

After draining the beer and sitting that can on a side table,
   and hearing the last of plucked Harry Lime
   doing its fade-out to momentary radio silence,
I carried the purple bag of plastic bottles to the door,
   pushing it gently but only slightly more ajar,
and heard water whoosh as she rose up in the tub
   and then splash a bit as she sat immediately back down.

> "Listen, Stevie," she called in that echoing voice, "there's no rug here right now and I don't want to step wet out of the tub and then slip and fall. Just put a hand over your eyes and bring it in, would you, please?"
>
> "You sure?"
>
> "Don't be embarrassed. Remember as actors we have to get used to such things. Don't feel uncomfortable. I'm not. Just keep your eyes closed. Promise?"
>
> "Sure," I said.

No way she needed to ask me twice on this,
   the violin theme from 'Out of Africa' now beginning,
and joining that theme I pushed open the door like waltzing,
   and in I plunged one hand over my eyes,
   feeling immediately the humidity all about me,
my bare feet on the hard tile now a little slick
   and therefore was I careful now feeling my way,
   calling on my foot-work skills as a high school shortstop,
and several times for a joke opening and closing my fingers quickly
   like camera shutters, although keeping eyes closed as promised.

> "Very funny, Stevie," she said in ironic voice. "Step a little closer."

My eyes closed like that, it just thrilled me the way she said my name,
   the timbre of her voice though deeper toned
   blended melodically with the 'Out of Africa' violins,
     (and how do you explain that phenomenon?—
     because I was a sappy 18-year-old of course
     all of this new to me, so much at once),
and stepping closer I felt the bag taken from my hand,
   and heard a baggy noise as she withdrew the plastic bottles,
then the noise of the bag hitting the tile floor near my feet.

"Would you please put that bag, Stevie, on the chair by the door."

"Sure," I said hearing her unwrap a bar of soap.

(Turning from her I opened my eyes, seeing the upholstered chair, never occurring to me why she had a chair in her bathroom. I turned back to her, again my hand over my eyes.)

"What is that music?" she asked.

(I told her.)

"It's beautiful."

"I have a friend, Mary, who can play violin like that."

"The one you accompanied this morning."

"Yes, exactly. She loves this intro."

"Lucky you—" (A moment's pause)— "better yet," said Scarlett, "instead of you shouting through the door, just turn that chair around and sit facing the wall and we'll talk. Put the bag in the sink."

"Not over my head," I said.

"No," she said, "not yet," by her tone obviously smiling.

Laying on the sink at that moment was a back-scrubber brush,
   and I laid it across the faucets to put that purple bag in the sink.
Though the mirror was a bit steamed I could see her in it opaquely,
   on her head a silly blue shower cap,
   and soap suds on her and all around her, even her shoulders,
that violin music echoing some in her bathroom,
   and her certainly the most beautiful woman I had ever laid eyes on.

The smell of eucalyptus hovered everywhere about me,
   but I wasn't sure if it were her soaps,
or possibly was it one of my olfactory hallucinations.

"How about this," I said.

*(I sat down astride that upholstered chair,
my back to her and a cushiony feeling under my ass.)*

"Yes that works perfectly. Have you ever done any acting before, Stevie?"

*(I could hear her moving about in the water,
and all this was intoxicating of course—
Scarlett, the music, and the aroma of eucalyptus,
now joined by that of lilac—
and me having had no lunch but coffee,
that one beer now began to take effect on me,
an 18-year-old's metabolism.)*

"No, no acting before," I said, "except some crap in grammar school, me Christopher Columbus if you can imagine that."

*(The humidity was getting me some, my shrugging
and pulling at the collar of my pullover.)*

"Have you got a T-shirt on under your pullover, Stevie?"

"No."

"Well, go ahead and pull it off anyway. It's pretty humid in here. I can understand."

*(It was definitely a huge relief to take it off,
my wiping my face and shoulders with it,
then laying it over the back of the chair,
and hanging my Giants' cap there as well.)*

"It's okay," she said. "As actors were going to have to be around each other in various states of dress. It's just part of the business. Don't pay it any heed. As actors we just have to get used to such things."

"I don't know why you say that, Scarlett. I'm not gonna *be* an actor."

"Now don't *say* that, Stevie, and block your mind. Most of the people in this studio will never be professionals. So just don't set your mind yet completely against it. You can't blend in if you block yourself. Maybe you might be. You never know. Life *does* have a strange way of twists and turns."

"Okay, that's a definite maybe," I said trying to be a little bit clever.

My back to her like that was frustrating like a blindfold,
   except was the medicine cabinet to my right and the mirror clearing,
so that with a bit of a lean and leer I could see her reflection,
   her sitting in a huge clubfoot tub, its own niche in the wall,
     plus its own showerhead and a curtain to draw around it,
her face so lovely even with that silly sky-blue cap on,
   and the top of her shoulders too with lovely slope,
but all else covered in bubbles and foam.

She had pulled the shower curtain half around the tub on the wall side,
   and her there against its navy blue background color,
it made her seem a single figure in a Punch and Judy puppet show.

Taking a deep breath I smiled accordingly,
   like the college sophomore I was then, or about to be,
and totally unsure of myself, uncharted waters,
   but not *that* nervous, not with her,
     my just not wanting to fail her.

The lilac aroma was slowly coming dominant,
   and for me now, unlike Ol' Walt,
were lilacs first in this doorway blooming.

"You like bubble baths, I take it, Scarlett," I said.

(I had to say something hearing her moving in the water.)

"I'm not addicted to them, no, not like some women, the Bubble Women."

"The Bubble Women?"

(That got me a good smile and laugh.)

"Yeah, they're full of illusions and they find bubble baths soothing."

"I see."

"Women come in many different colors and flavors, Stevie," she said, her voice not exactly enthusiastic.

"And men don't?"

"No, not nearly so many. We're all individuals of course, if we choose it, but men have bigger groups and fewer of them than women do."

"Okay, what's a male group off the top of your head?"

"The warrior kind."

"Oh wow," I responded.

> *(That truly stunned me to the core,*
> *given my obsession with Taranis,*
> *the 'warrior kind' not your everyday category.)*

"That's not exactly equivalent to Bubble Women," I said.

> *(I said that just to say something,*
> *anything, other than 'what the fuck!')*

"Ah, an equivalent. That would be 'pipe-dreamer.'"

"Pipe-dreamer?"

"Yeah, a guy who says he wants to be something but not doing anything to make it happen. Like a guy says he wants to be a musician but doesn't practice or cuts them to minimum. Or a guy who says he wants to own a business but doesn't take business courses because they're boring, and then says they're not necessary."

"Pipe-dreamer," I said. "That's not exactly the warrior kind."

"You bet. I knew a guy in college said he wanted to be a writer, was out every day experiencing life, or so he said, but never wrote, not a word, not even a journal. That'll come later, he said. Absolute pipe-dreamer."

"I understand," I said. "If you ain't doing it today, you ain't doing it tomorrow."

(That was a direct Monsignor quote for us altar boys.)

"Yes, exactly, Stevie. What's that from?"

"From the Monsignor, my pastor in grammar school."

"No, no, I mean that music playing now?"

"It's a song from *High Noon,* a Western. You ever seen it?"

"No. I like that though, do not forsake me oh my darling."

"Yeah, the whole movie takes place in a couple of hours his wedding day."

"His *wedding* day?" she said to verify.

"Yep, his refusal to turn his back on his people in the face of some truly significant bad guys. The irony is that all his people end up turning their backs on him, even his brand-new wife. That's why he's saying do not forsake me, because he won't be a coward and run away from what he feels is his duty as a man, a lawman, even if it kills him. Very Western."

"What's the matter with *her*?"

"She's a Quaker."

"Of course. How's it turn out?"

"I'm not saying. I hate people giving away movies. I've given away too much already. You might see it. I'd watch it with you. Great acting. Academy Award I think. Great western."

(I waited a few moments for that song to end.)

"It's that wail there at the end that gets me," I added when the song was over and commercial coming on. 'Wait a long…wait a long'…he's really torn between a rock and a hard place, love and duty and all that. Knowing the story that wail always gets me."

"Yes," she said behind me, "I see what you mean. You're sure are full of surprises. Oh nuts! "

"What?"

(My head soaring with her complement and the silence of no music I heard her turning in the water even some spilling out of the tub.)

"My back brush," she said. "I don't see it here on the floor."

"It's on the sink," I said.

"I must be getting old, my mind is going."

"Oh yeah," I said wryly, "that's gotta explain it."

"Be that as it may," she countered, "would you please hand it to me too."

"I understand," I said. "We actors can't abandon each other."

"Funny boy," she said. "Close your eyes."

(Not wanting her in any way angry with me I did it, "closed my eyes with brush in hand and did it, to her in the tub, moving toward her hesitantly, a Mr. Clean jingle ironically from Bose.)

"Just a little closer," she said.

(I inched towards her, feeling spilled water under my bare feet, Mr.Clean fading away quickly, and the new music beginning was as ironic as the commercial just over— the song from 'Summer of 42.')

"Oh what the hell, Stevie," she said, "you're already here. I'm going to turn my back. Would you go ahead and scrub it for me please. Actors have to get used to these things anyway."

*(... The summer smiles, the summer knows,
and unashamed she sheds her clothes...)*

So naïve, so country corn callow was I that this was first moment,
   absolutely first moment it occurred to me she might be seducing me,
my thoughts stimulated by the words of that song and theme of that film.

Yet still was I torn, not wanting to blunder,
   every one of you hearing this no doubt shaking your heads.

She *was* a worldly woman to me, so sophisticated,
   and I thought maybe that's just the way of such people,
maybe her truly dead serious about this just being actors,
their sometimes finding themselves in awkward positions,
   and her assuming me equally as sophisticated as her.

I heard the swish of her turning in the water,
   and now really the lilac aroma filling my nose.

...she sees the doubts within your eyes...

Opening my eyes I saw her back entirely bare,
   her arms embracing herself for modesty,
   and her in that silly sky-blue shower cap,
my hands unsure and my heart beating like a cannonade.

"Here take this soap, Stevie," she said softly, almost a whisper.

*(She had a bar in one hand held over her shoulder,
   from which the lilac aroma was arising.)*

"Rub it on me then scrub it for me if you'd be so kind. Gently at first."

"No problem," I said, nothing clever from my mind to add.

Because of the water on the floor,
   was I carefully stepping in my bare feet,
and using my previous shortstop experience
   to balance on my feet without slipping,
an action which she was no doubt sensing.

...twists the world around her summer finger...

"Sorry about no rug on the floor for slipping," she said. "It's actually in the damper. I washed it this morning."

Trying to reach the soap from her hand
   I did slip slightly, brush in my other hand,
quickly grabbing the rim of the tub instead of her soap,
   the rounded smooth enamel of it seized in my fingers.

"Oh dear, forgive me, Stevie," she said. "This isn't working so well, is it. Just go ahead and step in the tub to do it...no, no, you can't do that without getting your trousers soaked."

*(She went silent for a moment
as if she were giving it thought.)*

... And if you've learned your lesson well...

"Okay, okay," she said, "just go ahead and slip your trousers off and step in behind me. It's my own fault for putting you in this position."

"It *is* easy to slip and fall out here," I said.

"I know it's awkward. Forgive me, Stevie."

"We actors have to take care of each other," I said.

Truth is I was so adolescent that even then I wasn't certain,
   not certain at all if this were seduction or not,
     especially her in that silly shower cap,
but more was I just putting my adolescent faith in her,
   however this went.

Levi's and underwear slipped off and kicked aside,
   her leaning forward and gripping the other end of the tub,
I stepped behind her into that ocean of bubbles and suds,
   already the embarrassment of a hard-on I could deep-sea fish with.

...one last caress... it's time to dress... for Fall...

In that hard tub I went to my knees,
    mostly to conceal that rod in the water and bubbles,
    taking the soap from her hand reaching behind her,
and holding it very carefully like a loaded weapon
    I began sudsing her back with my hand and then brushing.

        "Oh yes, Stevie, yes," she said sensually, "oh that's so great, just
        a little more to each side…Oh yes, yes, that's it… ooh yes, you've
        got it. That's it…ooh, yes, that's it exactly."

        (Her head was bowed as I was brushing her,
        but suddenly she gasped and raised up.)

        "Oh dear, I'm getting a bit of a cramp in my leg. Close your eyes.
        I have to turn around and stretch it out."

Quickly she turned to me but I did not close my eyes,
    just leaned back on my haunches holding the brush and soap,
and suddenly there she was, her great face and shoulders,
    and her lovely breasts a bit soapy and sudsy,
    something like a foamy négligée around her,
and then her leg stretching out beside me,
    a bit of a grimace on her face,
but still so beautiful, even in that sky-blue shower cap.
I don't know whether it was my total gullibility,
    or me unconsciously improv-ing a scene from a movie,
but that bar of soap just spurted from my hand,
    shooting up in the air and splashing down between us,
and my eyes had to be as wide as saucers.

        "I'll get it," she said.

Now was she smiling, the cramp apparently stretched out,
    both her legs now going beside me in the tub,
and my kneeling perfectly still as into the water she dipped her hand,
    and of course seeking and finding my hard dick,
but no flinch from her, none at all,
    and not from me either, our eyes totally into each other's,
and once again she smiled at me trusting her.

Now not only lilac but heather and rose aromas filled the air,
    and which was real and which was not,
    no way I could possibly say at that moment,
me on my knees in the hard tub and water.

"Oh dear," she said, "what have I done?"

"Actors do that," I said to say something.

"And not just actors," she said, her fingers along my dick as if to verify her finding. "Not if the population of the world be any criterion."

That great voice and her green eyes large on mine and crinkling,
   was I gushing nervous a moment or two, but no fear really,
my eyes equally on hers, just total faith in her,
   a woman I had met but an hour before,
and then her hand goes softly over my dick like a glove,
   sending a rolling shudder up my spine,
   bursting out my through eyes with an adolescent's gasp.

"Ooh that's a hard one," she said.

*(She sucked air through pursed lips,
her eyebrows going up.
Me, I gasped again, this time voluntarily,
sucking air myself as she had done,
and that made her smile even more.)*

"You'd better stand up and come with me," she said.

"Are you sure," I said, my concern still locked on her slipping and falling.

"Of course I'm sure. Actors never abandon other actors in their time of need."

(Now huge smile on her face.)

"You're just so…beautiful," I said as explanation, but not excuse.

*(As it turned out I had stumbled on the perfect thing
   to say, and the perfect tone to say it in.)*

"Stand up with me, Stevie, we're gonna have ourselves an adventure."

"I've already started," I said.

(She loved that and actually laughed.)

"Come on, stand up with me."

"I…uh…I…uh…"

"Oh, come on, I've seen 'em before."

"Not mine," I said, though still letting her easily draw me up.

Leaning against me she turned on the shower as we stood,
   a single handled dial to do it with,
then a cold water shock for only a moment,
   making us both shudder and gush to the chill,
followed by a soft rain like shower upon us, perfect temperature,
   then her hand touching my dick with the warm water,
me as hard as ever, that's for sure, unaffected by the chill.

     "Apparently that's not going to do it," she said, like oh dear,
       trouble ahead.

After Scarlett turned to draw the shower curtain totally around us,
   the soft shower then washed the bubbles and soap off both of us,
her with a single twist of her hand stooping then to turn it off,
   and flipping off at the same time that sky-blue cap to hang on the dial,
her shaking her hair to roll down red over her shoulders and breasts,
   with that navy blue privacy no one else in the entire world but us,
just the two of us standing together totally naked,
   the second time only I had been so in my life with a woman.

     "Oh my," I said, like seeing a magician's magnificent illusion.

Both her hands went gently to my cheeks,
   my hands under her hair down and filled by her breasts,
soft and warm and pliable, and so totally alien to me,
although something like two brand-new licking puppies,
   an experience had as a kid at my Uncle Tom's ranch,
   watching over their birth with him, me totally then amazed,
as I was again totally now standing with Scarlett,
   except me this time a hard-on to hammer a 10 penny nail.

"You're kind of beautiful yourself, kiddo," she said. "Oh yes, definitely an adventure, and here's where it starts. You carefully step out and help me step out too. It *is* slippery without those rugs."

"Are they really in the dryer?"

"You *are* a quick study. No, they're in the closet over there."

Me out of the tub extending my hand to her carefully,
   her shrugging actually shyly now standing naked and alone.

"After all, I had to get you in the tub with me," she said.

Now I went shortstop again, conscious of my footwork,
   creating absolute stability to help her out safely,
   even taking her in my arms and she let me do it,
trusted me actually, us both nearly the same height,
   her now soft and luscious against me physically,
an immediate contrast to her certain mind and mysterious self.

"Well, well," I said, her now in my arms, "I see you're a natural redhead."

Still nervous am I of course, but not tongue-tied or thoughtless,
   and she gives me a shrug and smile to my observation.

The theme music just beginning is from 'Chariots of Fire,'
   that synthesizer opening electric constant beat,
   something like the thumping shaft of a ship full speed.
She hears it too and sucks air through pursed lips.

"What is *that*?"

"Chariots of Fire," I say.

"Only appropriate," says Scarlett.

(It is totally strange, even mysterious,
a completely new experience for me,
both of us standing there totally naked,
but yet at that point looking at each other,
neither of us particularly nervous,
especially not me anymore.)

"Come with me, Stevie." She takes my hand. "Actors don't abandon each other when things like this happen."

"Wait a long, Scarlett," I half sung, letting her take me.

Like I said I had placed all my faith in Scarlett,
   a woman met but an hour before.

Hurrying behind her, holding her hand,
   hearing the Chariot of Fire keyboards at beginning of that theme,
I see myself as one of those actors running in that opening scene,
   except of course they are not alone, nor with a beautiful woman,
stark naked both of us and her so beautiful,
   all of her…hair, face, knocks, and figure too,
   not to mention as fine an ass as Mary's for sure,
graceful too and athletic to boot.

She guides me by hand back into her bedroom,
   her other hand cradling her breasts,
and the afternoon sun pours itself through those windows,
   me down suddenly on her bed and startled again,
the beautiful colorful ageless art overhead in sunlight
   stunning me briefly before Scarlett stuns me more,
me totally enraptured by all of it,
from that can of Coors to radiant awesome beauty,
   both of ancient art and Bay Area skyline,
   but especially this red-headed sorceress,
my not knowing what to do, no idea at all,
   just my faith in Scarlett like a magic carpet.

She smiles, her face beautiful too in that sunlight,
   her kneeling beside me on the bed,
   her breasts kind of gawking at me now,
and at that moment suddenly a small panic,
   my remembering my wallet still in the bathroom,
but almost as if she is reading my mind,
   her other hand reaches into the drawer behind her,
   right where the empty Coors can stands,
and a condom packet is secured already half opened,
   which she now finishes off with her teeth,
   blowing a piece of that wrapper dramatically on the floor,

and amazes me her able to draw out that condom one hand and teeth,
  the Chariots of Fire rising up to its inspiring bridge.

… Quickly, efficiently, that condom is on me,
  with simple stroke of her hand as she purses her lips,
  and no doubt my eyes as wide as pies…

… Easily, athletically, and certainly gracefully, she slides under me,
  all arms, hands, and legs,
  just rolling me over on top of her,
  and me I'm sure sucking air…

… And then the marvelous wonder in me,
  always the same wonder every time with her,
  her legs spreading open under me,
  spreading open for *me,* only me,
  a wonder for me always and always…

… A little guidance of her hands,
  followed by a graceful and even artful movement of her hips,
  and virtually miraculously I am in her,
  the lubricated condom doing its thing,
  my dark eyes no doubt like wide black holes in space,
  that synthesizer piano sailing into its thrilling many-voiced bridge
  my meeting her hips as they rise up to me,
  and then impulsive my lower body seized by passion…

… Closing my eyes I leaned forward on my elbows,
  no experience ever before matching this,
  my cheek going beside hers to put my tongue in her ear,
  what I was told the thing to do at such a moment…

… But quickly has Scarlett my face in her hands,
  shaking my head to open my eyes,
  her eyes so green in the sunlight…

…"What are you doing," she whispers, not questioning but leading … "I, uh… "Focus, Stevie, what are you doing?"… *(my face in her hands, her eyes on me, the synthesizer music soaring and inspiring an image again of men running pell mell on a beach)*… "I'm fucking you," I declare… "Yes you are"... "Oh, beautiful Scarlett, I'm fucking beautiful Scarlett... "Yes you are, oh yes... God Almighty, Scarlett so beautiful and smelling of lilacs, I'm fucking Scarlett... Who are you fucking?...*(a shake of my head in her hands)*... "You, you, I'm fucking you"... *(I can feel myself smiling as broad as her in the sunlight...* "You, you, I'm fucking you, lilacs and you so beautiful"... "Yes, you are, oh like a horse you are, I'm being fucked, yes I am, I'm being fucked... *(me panting and gasping the music still soaring in my head, her hands on my face all this while and she sees and feels me going now, her breasts jiggling, her hips now easily meeting mine, me like plowing Mother Earth and I begin to shudder)...* "Yes, yes Stevie, there you go. Oh, I'm being fucked by a passionate boy with his dick so hard"... *(now from me are sounds and shouts of my coming, my shouting "Scarlett! Scarlett!"... (my going now from a sensual soaring to some kind of thrill of triumph, to a wondrous warm spirit swirling all around me)....*

"Oh my God, Scarlett, you're so soft and b-e-e-a-a-u-u-t-i-ful, Scarlett!...Scarlett!"...

"Yes, yes, and so you go, my beautiful boy, my beautiful, beautiful dark-eyed boy. So you go."

After Passion

The Chariot's theme had actually beaten me to climax,
    but not by much because I had been hurrying,
hurrying like those athletes on the beach at its beginning,
    a total of four minutes as I determined later,
but what a four minutes in my life.

People have run a mile in less time than that,
    or others a thrilling roller coaster ride,
but me I pushed through the outer doors
    and into the vestibule of masculinity,
but only the vestibule—
    hard lessons still to be learned.

Whether by her hands guiding me,
    or me just losing my balance,
over I went on my side,
    still inside her, still spurting some into that condom,

and when I opened my eyes, her eyes were still on me,
    her one hand still on my cheek, her face close,
so close she actually rubbed noses with me,
    huge expression of accomplishment on her face.
"Oh, oh," she smiled, "I'm being fucked."

I started to laugh as someone does affectionately teased,
    and that moment I realized, absolutely first time ever—
that above all else sex is fun,
    …lesson learned from the Great Scarlett Femi,
who sometimes called herself the Whore of Babylon.

Finding My Way

"You didn't come, did you?" I said.

"Not like you, that's for sure."

"But anything at all?"

"You have to understand, Stevie, what I do kinda stifles that. It's been a while for me."

"You do kinda like me, don't you," I said.

"Ya think!"

"It's just you're so beautiful," I said again, a kind of awe.

"Yes, I am," she said, startling me, so straightforward, "and it's a good thing for me. It opens doors. But that's all it does, open doors, and it's a lot of work and expensive too, being beautiful, but it does open doors, no doubt about that…and maybe even some I don't want opened."

> *(She patted my face with a smile,*
> *both of us naked under her satin sheets)*

"But don't let it throw you that I didn't come like you," she said. "Doesn't mean I didn't have a good time."

"What a *geek* I was."

"You're what, 18? Don't worry about it. It was fun."

So ironic it was startling was the music that began that moment,
   the thrilling overture to 'Gone with the Wind,'
      Tara's Theme— 'My Own True Love,'
with its huge symphonic power both beginning and end,
   as well as its moments of lull in between,
      making speaking easy without raising our voice,
and instantly at same moment did we both recognize it,
   bringing easy and warm smiles to our faces,
a kind of comic wash at the end of our passion,
   just as was amorous our soft shower after that soapy bath,
and I was delighted with its giving us extra time together.

"You know," she said, "they were gonna name me Charlotte."

"Really! My favorite aunt is named Charlotte."

"Yeah, but my mom was reading that book through her pregnancy and found herself all alone by circumstances at my birth. She just got confused postnatal and told the nurse 'Scarlett.' Sure surprised my dad when he got there finally."

"My favorite aunt," I said. "I call her Aunt Charlie."

"Same thing probably would have happened to me," said Scarlett. "Could you imagine me Charlie?"

   (I shook my head with complete certainty.)

"No, no way," I said. "No way you could ever be Charlie. Boggles my mind to even think about it."

"It pleases me you see that."

"It pleases me that pleases you. You *do* kind of like me then," I said again, more verifying than anything.

"I do, or you wouldn't be where you are right now."

"A dark-eyed boy," I said.

"Absolutely," said Scarlett, "a beautiful dark-eyed boy, and no doubt who your sister is."

The Power of Affection

"You kinda seduced me, Scarlett" I said.

I was saying anything to keep this moment going,
   the sound of her husky voice so tantalizing,
   the feel on my naked flesh of her soft satin sheets,
plus all the sensuality had thrilled me that afternoon,
   the soapy bath, the sex, the maze of my callow staggering,
   the eye filling shock and awe of her nakedness,
     both the bubble kind and the Eden variety;

and 'Gone with the Wind' now nearing its end,
   the thrilling romance of those horns and violins,
   all rising symphonically to its mighty climax,
one that had thrilled worldwide audiences for 50 years,
   including my sister, and me beside her,
   when I was nine years old and mostly bored—
I just wanted it to keep on going,
   even with that full condom still attached to my dick,
thus my saying first thing came to my mind.

   "You kinda seduced me, Scarlett."

   "Duh!"

   "What a rube I was," I confessed, feeling myself perfectly safe to do so.

   "You *were* a little bit slow on the uptake," she said, "but it was fun doing the baby step cha-cha."

   "Maybe I should be angry."

   "Oh yeah, right."

      (She put a hand to my cheek again.)

   "Ooh, ooh," she teased affectionately, "Scarlett, you're so beautiful."

   "Well, maybe I didn't mean it."

"And maybe I'm a Martian."

    ... My own true love fading on the violins...

"Are all guys like that," I said chagrined.

"Only the good ones."

    (That just totally left me relaxed and satisfied,
    my totally delighted by her close company.
    Still laying on her side she again patted my cheek,
    that white satin sheet under her arm and over her chest.)

"I've never been with anybody like you," I said, "no matter how you look at it— no one so beautiful, no one so sophisticated, the experiences you've had in your life, nobody like you. Ever!"

(She didn't say anything, just enjoying my experience of her,
maybe some things she still needed to do that day,
and me just wanting to hold on to the moment..)

"I guess I wasn't much of a lover," I said finally.

    (That was a question I had to ask at some time,
    and no use beating about the bush, so to speak.)

"Nothing coy about you," she said.

"Sometimes you just gotta step up and swing."

"Do you play baseball too?"

"I did in school."

"What position?"

"Shortstop."

(The closeness of her naked to me under that sheet,
and the faint aromas still remaining of lilac and heather,
the long fadeout of 'Gone with the Wind',
was such that I had to reach out and touch her shoulder
and then snatch my fingers away quickly.)

"I'm real," she said smiling.

She was delighting I think in me callow like that,
   not many like me anymore in her life,
probably only me, the naïve guy just wants to have fun.

Realizing that, I just about threw my arms around her,
   some fantasy of protecting her, or maybe the music,
but I quickly restrained myself from that silly gesture.

The last one in the world to protect Scarlett,
   and I mean the absolute last—
that would be me, and sobering that was
   and actually painful.

"Tell me, Stevie, how many girls you been with like this?"

*(This was a kind of 'scripted improv,'
a common scene in movies and theater,
and I just went with it.)*

"Only four or five."

"How many?"

"Okay, okay, just a couple."

"How many?"

"All right, only one… In Mexico."

*(She went silent, as had now
the stereo for the moment.)*

"Did you have a good baseball coach?"

"Huh… oh yeah, a great coach, Mr. Senelli."

"Tell me, Stevie, how would you have done in baseball without anyone coaching you at all or any experience either, and someone hands you a bat and says step up kid, be a man."

*(I smiled at that, getting her point,
my lips but a few inches from hers,
the FM now on commercial for used cars.)*

"I'd hit a home run," I boasted, like a man who had done it many times.

(She looked at me with squinting eye.)

"I'd strike out flailing," I admitted, "like I did in Mexico."

"I heard about that. Apparently it broke your heart."

*(On my side I nodded with a shrug—
what was there to say.)*

"I loved her," I said.

*(She looked at me a few moments,
like a talent scout evaluating.)*

"You want to know the truth?"

"Always," I said without hesitation.

*(She nodded to my tone, and I
could see her impressed by that.
That of course pleased me.)*

"Are you sure you can take it?"

*(I could feel this a big moment between us,
and took a serious second or two to consider.)*

"From you… absolutely… no problem," I said, "from you I want complete honesty."

(Now she even evaluated again and responded.)

"You were not in love. You're a boy. You have to be a man to be in love. That's the Big Leagues and most boys never make it."

(That was a hard slap all right.)

"I wasn't in love?"

"That's what I'm telling you, Stevie. I see boys every day in their 30s and 40s never become men, no idea even what a man is. Can't be with 'em,... can't be in love with 'em... won't even try."

"But *you* know what a man is."

*(That was my demand for truth,
our lips still only inches apart.)*

"Oh yes," she said confidently.

"Can you teach *me*?" I said, again without hesitation.

*(Now she seemed to evaluate me one more time,
us lying there on her bed, me long since slid out of her,
but now with full condom still attached,
and me still unsure what to do about that,
the news now coming on, something about Reagan.)*

"That's a definite maybe," she said.

"Now who's being coy? Yes or no. No beating about the bush."

"Yes," she said looking me in the eye. "Yes, I can teach you."

*(My heart must've done a Mao Osaka
double axel inside my chest.)*

"But there are rules," she warned, "just like baseball."

Now she sat up on the edge of the bed,
   facing those great windows and their views on the world,
and like legerdemain she pulled a sheer thing out from under a pillow,
   swirling it now around her shoulders and tying it off,
my no idea it was even there,
   nor was it disturbed a whit by our passion.

"And the rules are hard and fast," she warned. "You understand?"

"No problem," I said.

"I'm the boss," she said, "always the boss. What I say goes when you're with me. You do what I tell you, about everything. You can't live with that then there's the door."

"Can I put my pants on first or do I have to streak into the elevator?"

(That gave her a bit of a laugh.)

"That would give Tommy a heart attack for sure."

(She turned back to me propped up on my elbow on the bed and reached her fingers again to my cheek.)

"Who's the boss?"

(I did not say anything.)

"Who's the *boss*, Stevie. Say it so there's no misunderstanding."

"You are," I agreed. "The boss of you, and what's around you."

"'Nuff said," she said. "That will work."

"…and there's the door and my pants are in the bathroom."

(Now she patted my cheek more firmly, imitating a movie mafioso.)

"You do like to have fun, kiddo," she said. "That's a really great instinct to build from."

I cannot describe the rush of hope took hold of me,
   and I swear it seemed by this one stroke
     the memory of Marlena and Mexico fell fully pacified,
and let me tell you the lesson learned from that—
   no one can abuse you more than your own damn self.

"Wow, Scarlett, I don't know what to say," I gushed. "This is… truly it's amazing…like the hand of God."

"Hardly," she scoffed, "more the hand of your sister. Don't blow it. Now go in the bathroom and flush that thing and go ahead and get your pants back on so we can talk."

"Yes, sir," I said with a screwy salute.

Just what she had ordered I hurried and did,
   including my Giants cap on as well,
and sat down on her left side,
   her still on the bed looking out the window,
her mind obviously in a different country.

The afternoon light was clear enough to see traffic on the bridge,
   plus several big ships in the Bay coming and going,
and she sat there with that sheer rosy thing tied around her,
   from which her breasts and womanliness just seemed to burgeon forth,
      (a word I've always loved— 'burgeon,'
      most especially for Scarlett the Beautiful).

"Is there hope for me, Casey," I pleaded dramatically. "Will I ever get a single?"

"A single!" she said, a look like I had farted.

(Now she put the back of her left hand to my cheek,
truly a surprising affection, regardless of the sex.)

"I'm gonna make you the Sultan of Swat," she said. "All you gotta do is listen and learn and stick to business."

    (I made an exaggerated gasp with expression
    of wide-eyed wonder and delight.
    Then she put her left arm around me,
    like my sister often did growing up,
    something else now on Scarlett's mind.)

"Don't get carried away," she said. "Sex ain't hardball, Babe. In fact it's pretty much slow pitch softball. A little instruction, a little practice, a little love and anyone can do it."

"If the population of the planet is any criterion," I said.

(She liked my remembering that.)

"But to do it well, oh Great One," I said.

"Ah, to do it well," she nodded, wagging her right index,. "That's a horse of a different color, isn't it?"

"What's it take to be that horse?"

"Confidence first, followed by energy and heart. But first must always be confidence."

"Pretty much like everything else worthwhile in the world," I said.

(Now she smiled again, that lovely Scarlett smile. She liked what I said. Wherever her head had been now she was back with me.)

"But there's more, Stevie," she said with a single wag.

"There always is," I said.

"Yes, Grasshopper," she said with mock Asian accent.

(But also was a single gesture of her index finger now, a gesture to let me know without question that important if not critical specifications about to be broached.)

"Always for good sex must be a sense of delight and gender mystery," she said airily, almost romantically, "plus a sense of direction"... *(this added with a deep tone of realism and eyebrows raised with caution)*...highly important that sense of direction... not to mention a willingness to be embarrassed and stylishly naked."

"Sheer gowns and bubbles," I said, and delighted was I that made her nod and smile.

"A quick study like I said," she said.

(Now she turned to face me directly.)

"But for the best sex, kiddo, the absolute best"…again her finger raised and dramatic pause, me on the edge of her bed waiting… "must be friendship and affection."

(That startled me, the last things I would think of.)

"Then what about love?" I countered.

"Ah, love," she said, the same way you might say, Ah, a unicorn, "Stick with friendship and affection and leave love for parents and children."

"What about looks?"

"Looks are pass/fail," she said, "and a huge gray zone there between them, especially for men, an ever changing gray zone."

(Something else occurred to me at that moment, and I started to fidget and look away.)

"What?" She said. "I'm telling you don't ever mix love and relationship."

"No, something else."

(My tone had turned serious, nothing comic about it, and no doubt she guessed why.)

"What," she said again, a more gentle tone, prodding me, waiting for me to broach it myself.

"You didn't say anything about…uh…you know… physique."

(She made something like a snort of disdain.)

"Men and their dicks," she said, sitting there on the edge of her bed and shaking her head.

"Come on," I said, "that's not fair. It's not like breast implants are a back alley business."

"Touché," she said, "but a world of difference between them."

She stood up now to her great windows,
    and I stood with her,
looking directly down at Chinatown below us,
    and then to the Embarcadero and the wharves and piers.

"You're more a man already than half the men I know."

"Really," I said pleased, wanting to believe her.

"Don't get huffy and puffy," she said. "It's likely because of your sister."

"Or my mother maybe."

(I could tell she liked I said that.)

"A definite maybe," she said.

Near the Ferry Building a huge cruise ship was backing out of a dock,
    soon to be under the Golden Gate and bound for the high seas,
    and would be out there long before the dark of the night and starry skies,
and just to its right stood the Bay Bridge, 'The Pride of Man,'
    something of a phallic symbol for sure.

Scarlett and I were about the same height,
    me a little taller in our bare feet.

"Listen now, Stevie. I'm only gonna say it this once," she began.

*(She was speaking not so much to me,
but mysteriously more like out at that bridge.)*

"When it comes to men and their dicks," she continued, "it's all pass/fail like looks."

*(Scarlett turned now her look to me, reading me, and me
like waiting for a term paper to be handed out,
to find out my grade, and sometimes shocked.)*

"Relax," she said. "Pass."

*(Now I went comical, wiping my fingers across my forehead,
and then leaning towards her for a little something extra.)*

"With flying colors?" I asked, dramatically hopeful.

"No," she smirked, "but pass. That's all you need."

*(My face must have been that of
a driver pulled over by a cop.)*

"Listen, Stevie," she said serious as a hypo, "Men and their big dicks. It's true small dicks can be a problem, specially less than 4 inches, but that can be overcome with friendship and affection. Relax, that's not you. The real problem is too *big*."

"Too big!" I said stunned, an unheard of concept.

"Absolutely. You get over 8 inches and it can *hurt*, especially someone no sense of direction, and anything over 9 inches is a curse, an interesting toy for a while but eventually a curse. Just *always* hurts."

"Wow," I said, "I had no idea."

"Just the reality of it," said Scarlett. "And guys with big dicks are usually assholes anyway. Don't know why. Probably genetic."

(No doubt to me she had someone in mind.)

"It must be Darwinian," I said. "Assholes being assholes, they don't get laid much so that's gotta thin the Big Dick herd and maybe that's a boon for women's comfort."

*(I didn't think that all that clever, but Scarlett
threw back her head and laughed out loud.)*

"Thin the big dick herd," she repeated, laughing,

(That of course pleased me.)

"And here's another odd thing," she said. "The size of your dick has nothing to do with your height, and big guys with average dicks, that makes them look smaller. That's where *you're* lucky."

"A shorter guy with a big dick," I offered.

"Come on, you know who you are. You pass, and your being shorter in height makes your dick look bigger. Gotta take it, the good with the bad, if that helps your ego."

(I threw back my shoulders, adjusting them like after a tussle.)

"M-m-y-e-a-h," I said with Philadelphia accent, "m-m-y-e-a-h it does."

"Men," she said, and not with flattery. "Lucky for you, Stevie, you're not the biggest or even close."

"Lucky?" I said.

"M-m-y-e-a-h," she said, smiling at me. "Trust me on that. You, you're very comfortable. M-m-y-e-a-h."

"Like an old shoe," I suppose.

"Maybe, but there *is* one thing really unique about you, and it's a *very* good thing as well."

"There is," I said with dramatic hopefulness again.

"M-m-y-e-a-h," she said, enjoying all this, "one of the benefits of sex in the afternoon."

(Now was I bewildered, trying to figure this one out, and she was letting me stew a bit.)

"What?" I said finally, no idea at all.

"I believe yours is the prettiest dick I have *ever* seen."

"The prettiest!" I said, not knowing what to make of that.

"Yes."

"Not the biggest?"

"No-o-o-o."

(I drooped my head and shoulders like Pinocchio in mock despair.)

"Oh, stop," she said with a smile, enjoying my impression. "As far as I'm concerned you should consider yourself head of the line when they handed out dicks."

> *(Now up came my head and shoulders,*
> *Pinocchio proud with smug face.)*

"Pretty," I said warming to that, "and you know this how?"

(Her voice took a tone both of surprise and realism.)

"Because I've *been* to the Land of the Giants, and the Island of the Ugly."

"Jesus, Scarlett," I said now, my comic self overwhelmed.

"Didn't your sister tell you what I do… Why I'm taking this acting class…or studio as they call it… Why I *need* you?"

"No, she just told me you're a professional woman, and one of her closest friends, and needed some help. And especially she told me she can only beat you half the time at tennis. That bugs her big."

> *(Scarlett smiled a huge smile of affection.)*

"She *is* a good friend for sure, but half the time, I-I-I don't think so. Close but no cigar. Come on, let's go have some coffee out in the kitchen. We need to talk more."

"You mean were all done in here?" I said sadly. "Practice makes perfect."

"Who's the boss?"

"You are, you are," I retorted, my hands in the air like a western movie. "I'll go peaceable, sheriff."

"See that you do."

"Oh," I sighed, shoulders slumped "to you I'm just another pretty dick."

She took my hand and squeezed it,
    liking that joke more than any I had said,
but for me as an 18-year-old,
    that afternoon tub and bed with Scarlett,
    that was a life changer as you might guess;
and when she had said that pretty dick thing,
    her tone seeming so totally sincere,
    and here's me of course believing it to this day,
but whatever it was, rumplesnitz or truthfulness,
    it sure did work well for me,
    me never a shower room stalwart,
        certainly not like my good friend Sean Coughlin.

The truth also is I have heard that again, "pretty dick,"
    and from one especially important to me,
such that I gave thanks to a guy never met,
    the one who had done my circumcision,
apparently should've been an artist,
    or at the very least a plastic surgeon.

And Scarlett was so right about friendship and affection—
    those two do always create the hottest sex… always…
and certainly by far the most satisfying,
    a light year at least and maybe more
    beyond the mutual masturbation most sex is—
although any port in a storm has a certain value,
    yet too often brings only long-term loss…
another lesson learned from the Great Scarlett Femi.

Trust

In the kitchen over coffee Scarlett trusted me—
    can't say why exactly or what I had done,
more I think she just decided she needed to trust somebody,
    and I was the closest one pass/fail that served her purpose.

She pretty much laid out for me her professional life,
    $1000 minimum and she's your constant companion that night,
and will enhance your status with beauty, grace, and charm,
    not to mention an intellect engaging and quick;
or create soirées for your business or just doubles for tennis,
    and tennis can be career critical, believe it or not,
far and away more so than golf, said Scarlett,

and golf a game she did not care for,
not nearly enough huffing and puffing for her tastes.

She laid all this out for me, without any shame or embarrassment,
    our drinking coffee from beautiful Salvador Dali pedestal cups,
and several of his works uniquely emblazoned on each cup,
    and purchased I learned as a pair at the Renaissance Fair,
    and apparently quite expensive,
but she just loved them for some reason,
    maybe not as impressive as her bedroom ceiling,
    but truly they must be a treasure, I said to her,
her replying, "Hell, yes they are."

I must say not really shocked was I to hear her tale of herself,
    actually was I more impressed, though still intimidated some,
and why was she even bothering with the likes of me,
    pretty much wasting her valuable time.

Then she told me what she was looking for,
    looking me in the eye to do so,
trusting me if not like a friend,
    then at least the ally needed to change her life.

She badly wanted out of her current way of being and life,
    just no future in it beyond 30.

She had to either work long enough to permanently retire, *(but then what?)*,
    or find an alternate life style that suited her talents,
    a style that could carry her further into life;
and there was another good friend who believed in her too,
    that friend being my sister,
believed in Scarlett's talent and energy and spirit,
    and was therefore encouraging her into this Acting Studio,
    opening the door into acting, especially theater acting.

But only opening it was she, all she could do,
Scarlett needing to push on through it,
    like me that day in pursuit of manhood,
    pushing an open the door into her bathroom,
and this my place in our mutual aid pact,
    my helping her by keeping the wild dicks off her,
    as she focused on her bridge of escape.

In return she would open the door and guide me
   into an experienced and enjoyable masculinity.
But she was the boss, she said,
   she was Casey Stengel, or Vince Lombardi,
and was I man enough to live up to that deal?

> "Sex is one thing, Stevie," she said, "but this is life I'm talking about now, and the question is are you man enough already to look me in the eye and live up to that deal."

> *(I took a dramatic sip of coffee from that beautiful cup.)*

> "How do I show you I'm man enough," I said. "Do I spit in my hand to shake with you, or patty cake maybe, or how about kissing your ass or mooning you?"

> "Just have the conscience to see it truly because I need your commitment here and no sudden sayonara or appointment in Samarra."

> *(I loved that, almost a couplet from Alexander Pope,*
>   *'no sudden sayonara or appointment in Samarra'.*
>   *My GrammaKate would have loved that too.)*

> "You're offering me an entry into you," I said.

> "There's truth to that," she said, "in more ways than one."

> "I don't need time," I said. "I got the time. My dance card is open until August. No other commitment. Of course I'll do it. You knew that already back at the restaurant or you would never have brought me here to your Fortress of Solitude."

> "You are a quick study."

> *(Now was a long moment of silence,*
>   *our looking at each other over those*
>   *Renaissance cups, eye to eye,*
>   *this a huge moment in both our lives.)*

"Don't think twice, it's all right," I said. "I'm the boss of me. Of course I'll do it for someone like you, and don't worry I won't let you down."

> *(That was a huge statement and commitment.*
> *I needed something to convince her.*
> *I put down that cup and pointed to my eyes.)*

"Look at these eyes," I said. "These are Krayle eyes, the eyes of Cossack warrior blood, originally Kirilenko, and my grandfather was a bank robber and murderer in El Paso Texas, seriously Bad Bob Krayle, him and my grandmother both."

> *(That brought out a great Scarlett smile.)*

"Really, your grandmother too… really."

"Yes, GrammaKate. She just died two years ago, right after my 16th birthday. I was her favorite."

> *(Thinking now about GrammaKate stopped*
> *my pretentious pitch dead in its tracks,*
> *and altered my sense of self.)*

"I really miss her," I said. "You would have loved her."

"I love her already."

"I'll tell you about her as I remember things. She sure loved poetry. Gave that love to me. Had this great huge leather bound volume of poetry her husband had given her, her second husband, not Bad Bob Krayle, another guy, and he gave it to her when they first got married. She wanted me to have it after she died. I wish now I had kept it."

> *(This was reaching now into my heart,*
> *and I wasn't that far from tears.)*

"What did you do with it?" demanded Scarlett, upset my losing it.

"I buried it with her, tucked under her hand."

*(Now remembering GrammaKate and missing her,
her in her coffin that volume under her hand,
I started to cry, waving my right hand at Scarlett
to disregard it, then rubbing my eyes
with thumb and index of my left hand.)*

"Where was I?" I said after a moment.

"You were convincing me I can depend on you," she said with her beautiful Scarlett smile.

*(She leaned over and put a hand on my cheek
and I let her. How warm it felt.)*

"You succeeded," she said.

Women… they just put too much faith in tears.

<u>The End</u>

GrammaKate Fragment:

The Crotch Rocket

Highpockets is a woman who understands the metaphysics of river,
    and I cannot tell you why or how, perhaps just by instinct,
but river and consciousness, she taught me, are the same,
      one the image of the other,
only of course in separate realities, one mind and one matter—

The point is they both share the same dynamic,
    or so she said, and I accept it now,
and over the years since kids she has always said this,
      that river must come and it must go,
      and if it fails to do that, fails to keep that balance,
          it won't be river long.
The same with consciousness.

Therefore, to keep consciousness going and healthy,
    (and she swears she got this understanding from the Monsignor),
learning and teaching both are daily necessities,
      the two food groups of soul, you might say,
and probably that's the reason she was so patient that evening,
      both with Peter Aquitaine and especially with me.

But the irony is that learning requires more courage than teaching,
    or so I taught *her, (and I got that from the Monsignor as well)*,
and how right he was, the Monsignor, no question about it,
learning demanding a similar *(but not matching)* courage to risking your life
      because whatever you learn, whatever it is,
         from calculus to fiddle, from hopscotch to tag,
      whatever you learn you're never the same again,
         not the same person, the river moved on,
      and that can be scary, very scary indeed, even paralyzing.

Imagine Einstein before and after $E=MC^2$
    as heroic as Hercules, or Clark Kent to Superman;
or imagine Copernicus realizing the earth is spinning in a solar system,
      and only him alone knowing it until after his death,
      totally unable to teach it for fear of his life.
Just imagine that clog in the river that egregious imbalance caused,
      and the insanity for him that he must have borne.

It's the same for all of us, it seems obvious, the need to make balance,
   (but to a far lesser degree of course than Einstein or Copernicus).

And especially is it true between lovers,
   the need to teach and learn,
If you really want a dynamic relationship,
   and both of you howling at the top of your lungs,
then you got to teach and you got to learn.
But just remember, learning requires the more courage,
   and it just can't be one of you,
     it has to be both… must be both of you.

I surely could see this dynamic develop between HP and Aquitaine,
   their teaching each other,
and her no wallflower if you haven't gotten my drift yet,
   carrying her weight and more in any relationship,
   in any phase or nuance of human to human.

Just as he was teaching her art and sailing,
she was teaching him grace and movement—
   athletics and dance of course,
but first of all teaching him her first love, bicycling,
   (just ahead of tennis in her world).

It was not that he was geeky,
   in fact quite the opposite,
     since no true sailor can be geeky.
It was just not something he had pursued, athletics,
   not organized or regular since high school P.E.

Yet to be with her he had to be athletic,
   and to him, *(just as to me),*
     she was a woman of many mansions,
       and he wanted her, or at least part of her
         both in his life and in his heart, and probably forever;
   and to his credit he came to it easily, athleticism,
     just needing a little training and encouragement
     to bring out what was already there.

Perhaps the perfect analogy for him is photography,
   something he as an artist had minimally pursued,
but when their sailing adventures brought him to it,
   he became quickly productive with eye-popping creativity,

not just skillful but innovative and original;
and a life saver to them both, or so it would truly become,
    when her private misadventures cracked open their world,
        like a bad old Hollywood monster movie,
and truly up on her would come fearful devastation and slaughter,
    a human Kraken up and at her from the Heart of Darkness itself,
but I'll get to all that in due course.

Bicycle Then Motorcycle

When it came to cycling,
    me and her had ridden together over the years,
    ever since we were kids, up and down 24th Street to start,
and now with Aquitaine the three of us,
our riding not so much east of Twin Peaks,
    not towards downtown, because of the hills,
but towards the avenues instead,
    especially towards Golden Gate Park,
chasing each other through off roads and paths there,
    and then cycling out to the Great Highway along the ocean,
    cars whizzing by creating some fright and dilemma,
        but though giving us a certain thrill of danger,
        it was not really that dangerous at all,
            not in daylight hours,
    and only motorcycles causing us wince going by,
    the machine gun racket and roar of their motors alarming us.

And one time we took a full day,
    and went on a road trip across the Golden Gate to Sausalito,
    pumping hard through the heavy winds on the Bridge,
courteous and careful around the snugly coated tourists,
our coasting with polite "good day" and "excuse us,"
    the bay on the one side, the sightseer side,
        and on that side Alcatraz and Angel Island pointed to by all,
        sailboat sails and small craft too on that side skimming the waters;
but on the other side, the Pacific side, the crushingly hugely infinite side,
    nothing but waves and blue sea all the way to the horizon,
        and just steaming out under us to brave the abyss
        was a cargo ship with a deck full of orange and blue containers,
            the ship blowing its loud sea horn, heard up and down the bridge,
                (a horn sounding huge as a bassoon or tuba big as the Ritz,
                announcing three times its puny intentions to the infinite sea),
and that enormous conflict of size and magnitude between bay and sea

crushes the hopes of anyone clutched by lugubrious gloom or melancholy,
    and thus the north end of the Bridge a famous suicide launch.

But we three panting pedaled hard that day past all that,
    and then down into Sausalito on the water,
        very careful of course of traffic and trucks,
a beautiful little city now for tourists and sail boaters,
    (but a history too of rum running, whoring, and mayhem,
    and notorious murders from Roaring 20's through World War Two),
and obviously our bicycle trip there stimulated Aquitaine's thought,
    for two years later he moved himself and his entire art school there,
    which in effect would sever off his City consciousness,
        (something like Great GrammaKate herself moving with
        Billy Bob and her family to a farm in the Valley of the Moon
        and thus turning themselves alien to life in the City),
    a different world totally then for Aquitaine, a different way of life,
        crossed over the Bridge and out of the City,
        hard to describe it, just different sensibilities,
            no longer nurtured by City culture and consciousness;
and thus HighPockets began living in two separate worlds,
    each one distinct and separate from the other,
        one world Barbary Coast and the Naked City,
        and the other world Aquitaine, sailing, and art,
        and best never that twain should meet,
for Aquitaine truly had shed City-self and consciousness,
    although still a mind-set he could re-assume crossing back over,
    something like a Silkie he would say as a joke,
        taking human form to come out of the sea;
        and for a time after he moved to Sausalito
        he had taken to painting various images of Silkies,
            but mostly female ones and not always beautiful.

My sister being who she is,
    a magnificently organized mind,
she could manage well the 2 worlds separately,
    (something I could not understand until the Marines,
    and then of course I could not understand
    how it was I had not understood it.)

Incidentally after my Marine days and the killing we did then
    would come my motorcycle days and self-slaughter being,
        itself a totally different consciousness from those bicycle days,
and she loved to come ride with me on occasion, HighPockets,

both for herself and for me equally, I think,
   her sensing but not understanding the violent past within me,
      for I denied ever having been in battle or immersed in deadliness,
      shooting people up close or half a mile distant or more,
      or strangling PrettyBoy to death with my bare hands,
   no need for her or Mary or family or anyone to know any of that,
      and I just denied the killing, as GrammaKate had always done.

Me and HP rode around the entire City on my Harley,
   usually a similar ride each time
      on my neon purple Custom 88 Soft-tail,
      with gray flames painted either side of the purple tank,
      (my 'sickel' I called it because that was Widow's word,
      a word no other motorcyclist I ever knew used,
      just something I shared with him, with Widow,
      especially since originally this sickel had belonged to him).

First we'd ride around downtown after picking her up at the theater,
   but always on the sickle, us wide open like on a horse
   always did we feel encumbered by traffic and snarl,
the bus exhaust not only sickly but even abrasive to our noses,
   and the constant concrete hard assault on our flesh,
   or so it feels riding a motorcycle.

So we hightailed it out Pine Street to Masonic,
   squirreling around a bit to reach Fulton Avenue to Stanyan Hill,
   on past the Farroway Institute of course,
      her always giving them the finger,
         especially anyone seen in a white coat,
         the only time I ever saw her flip the bird;
and then to the left we went down Stanyan Hill,
   past St. Mary's Hospital and E.R.
   past the Panhandle and Oak street,
      where Aquitaine once had lived,
   then on past Haight Street and the park entrance,
but not yet going into the park,
   instead scooting up Stanyan to Parnassus Hill,
      her holding me tightly as we did so,
   past his Lordship the UC Hospital and its environs,
      the labyrinth for so many of bloody hope and hopelessness,
   zipping by Corbett Street, named for Gentleman Jim,
      the 2nd heavyweight champ of the world,
      who had grown up in San Francisco,

and where at that time my apartment would be located,
   its back up tight against the base of Twin Peaks…

then me thundering that sickle with HP up the winding Peaks' road,
   that Harley 4-stroker in signature deafening roar,
   sounding like a 50 caliber Ma Deuce machine gun,
     mowing men down like the Grim Reaper himself,
   HP hanging on tightly as we climbed…

and at the summit our running the figure 8's between the two peaks,
   usually past a Grey Tour bus or two,
   the buzz of vibration awakening all our bones,
   and HP's breasts up tight against me hugging me now,
     especially on warm days without need of jackets,
     her consciously or not relying on my brotherhood,
        and on my discipline as a Marine as well,
     to not become sexually excited,
        our leaning one way and then the other,
        swaying like dancers to and fro,
        running those figure 8's…

Then there on that Twin Peaks summit always we'd feel it,
   the chill in our faces, and thrill of the speed,
   that 4-stroker drilling and hammering between our legs,
   the roar in our ears, the buzz of our vibrating bones,
that true sickle high needing our endurance to reach it,
   and the rush of endorphins flushing through us
   causing that high and the grins on our faces,
     and for me that hallucinatory aroma of roses…

and leaning through those curves came glimpses down Market Street,
   a recurring flickering image east side of those curves,
   Market Street like an aorta all the way down to the bay,
     streaming streetcars and busses and busy humanity,
     all of it shoulder to shoulder, metal and flesh,
        like blood cells for a city I'd guess you could say…

Then back down the Peaks we'd roll, again to Stanyan,
   turning left into Golden Gate Park,
our riding calmly with courtesy now past the Hall of Flowers,
   past the one block Boulevard and Arboreal
     where the DeYoung Museum faces off the Hall of Science,
       and the Arboreal between them to isolate each experience,

the DeYoung the one she took me to 15 years old,
to confront first time that Great Oaf Libido that had seized me,
my staggering wide-eyed through the beauty there of artistic nudity,
    Old Master, modernist, or impressionist just didn't matter,
totally changing at age 15 my understanding of woman and nakedness…

and now over a dozen years later her with her arms tight around me
rolling through the Park, all smells again delightful,
    whether pine or eucalyptus or my private roses,
the green of the grass and stout-hearted trees and colorful flowers,
    something indeed like shattered pieces of a rainbow,
    and always like a bath for our fatiguing spirits,
        a common experience available to City folk in San Francisco.

Then out of the Park we'd dart,
    especially if we caught the stoplight,
to roar that vibrating frame down the Great Highway,
    the beach on our right of the infinite Pacific,
the buzz of Park and Peaks still in our bones,
    our passing cars, slipping in and out with impunity,
    her arms always around me tightly,
and always her unafraid and unconcerned,
      total faith in my reflex and judgment
      hammered and shaped by my Jarhead days,
        a fact she found unpalatable and disquieting,
        but right now relied on the safe truth of each,
           my reflex and judgment learned as a Marine,
        her arms around me tightly,
           and sometimes her helmeted head on my shoulder.

Occasionally when both of us had a full day's leisure,
    carefully outfitted in leather (me) and buckskin (her),
we'd ride north across the Bridge, past Sausalito,
    riding the freeway all the way to Santa Rosa,
        (East of Eden and the Valley of the Moon)
not only our birthplace but home to Luther Burbank,
    where he enlightened all our spirits from his flowery soul,
    the soft beauty of flora filling all his years,
        not weapons or marching orders,
        not gunsmoke, nor full metal jacket,
        nor Harley-Davidson with its unique roar
        that always reminded me of the roar of a warrior,
           (or a Ma Deuce spitting death near a 1000 rounds a minute)

   no, not for old Luther Burbank,
     always for him rainbow colors from burgeoning life...

our then taking the two-laner out of Santa Rosa,
  curving along the Russian River,
  darting in and out of sunlight,
    giving us moments of warmth and shivering chill,
    her hugging me close when the chilling seized her,
  me in my wrap around Ray-Ban sunglasses and full red helmet,
    yellow lightning bolts on the side,
  and her in blue half helmet and goggles,
    the sound of the wind sometimes screaming in our ears,
    even with the plugs we used for the ride...

and occasionally another cyclist fell in beside us,
  a lone wolf out for a howling run,
our rising and falling together on the rolling highway,
  leaning back and forth in and out of curves,
  rolling through Guerneville slowly and faster through Monte Rio,
then hightailing it and roaring after the fork in the road,
  not to Occidental but to Duncan Mills instead,
  past Magic Mountain on the right,
    where Mary's summer home stands atop it,
    and if she were there and looking surely she could see us
    running and howling along that gently rolling road...

Then a pleasant wave of our left hands
  to any cyclist who had joined us,
  when their journey carried them apart,
    no need for names or even words between us,
    something like eagles soaring and departing...

Out to Jenner-by-the-Sea we'd roar,
and usually by then her voice wild in my ear,
  the city restraints and Barbary Coast sentience
  now stripped away completely and flung aside for the time,
  and her just whooping and hollering all the way to Jenner,
    all along that rolling riverside road,
      rising and falling,
      her arms so around me...

At Jenner-by-the-Sea we turned south on Highway One,
  (that number so meaningful to me after my life in Spain, me and Mary,

and all my heart still in the heart of a Malagueña I knew there once),
our running the curves along the Pacific coast line,
   now certainly cooler and sometimes bone chilling,
      our leaning and swaying again together,
         first one way and then the other,
         speeding up or slowing down,
         like dancing or sailing
         or even sometimes like flying …

Motorists we passed were so frustrated by slow Coast Highway,
   half the cruising speed of any freeway,
yet us on 2 wheels, the wind in our faces, it made no difference,
   those pistons pounding and vibrating between our legs,
   depending whether faster or slower, straightaway or curve,
our hearts beating faster and slower themselves,
proclaiming to the universe the grandeur of it all,
   hard crag and mountain to our left,
   but below to the right and endlessly
      the foamy blue eternal abyss,
      Pacific infinite onliness stretching out beyond the horizon…

and we sailed along between those 2 sensibilities,
   hard rock and seawater,
as only sickle people understand,
   although sometimes rolling between 2 rocky rises,
      the sunlight vanishing a moment or two,
   caused us a moment's shudder again and bone shiver,
      HP hugging me even tighter,
   until back again into the open road,
      and again upon us the warm light fell,
the magnificence of it all thrilling us both,
   as it must have thrilled GrammaKate's heart
   on their Sunday sedan rides to this same blue sea,
      back in the 20's and 30's before Pearl Harbor,
      2 lanes only, no 4 lanes or freeways,
   in their eye-popping carmine colored Essex-Durant touring sedan,
   first with mamma in the back seat alone, and then the others,
      her family growing time to time,
      Uncle Christopher too, later killed in that war,
      even sometimes my dad with them and Uncle Tom too,
         neighbor kids as they were, invited along for the ride by the sea,
      and never during any of those years, never once,
         a single mention by GrammaKate of the name Bad Bob or El Paso,

and certainly the magnificence of it all thrilled her then like us this day...
Then on down the Coast Highway we rolled,
    me and HP on my Custom 88 purple Soft Tail Harley,
exploding piston racket and roar,
    causing sudden winces and angry faces
    on any angry bicyclists we blew by;
and each car driver eyed us,
    that sickle waltz by us,
all their thoughts prying at us,
    wishing and sighing at us,
especially the old men in a Byzantium moment,
    who had pretty plumage once;
as down we rolled through the pleasance of Bolinas,
    houses always reminded me of Widow Walkers by the sea,
    women waiting grimly for their men to return home safely...

And then sadly our adventure ending always at Stinson Beach,
    (breeding grounds of Great Whites, she once told me),
and always there a late lunch, indoors or out,
    our chatting excitedly,
for each ride, *(even when the exact same route),*
so marvelously different in magnificence,
    like a different turn of a kaleidoscope,
    and therefore so much to share and talk about,
        our grins and chatter and gleaming eyes,
        our helmets sitting on chairs beside us,
    and the other patrons always pleased by our passion,
        even perhaps coveting it...

After lunch the Soft Tail roared again,
    climbing up from Stinson then down to catch the freeway,
    past dull San Rafael and the ever placid north bay estuary,
speeding up over the coastal range, climbing again on the freeway,
    and then down once more toward the Golden Gate Bridge,
        always itself a splendid orange majesty below us,
        seen first in a glimpse as we skimmed over the summit;
and then the deafening echoing of our roar through the tunnel,
    both of us chilled to the bone again,
    and her seizing me close again tightly for warmth
        in that windy sunless chute of a tunnel,
our bursting out of it ironically like a bat out of hell,
and the Bridge again below us brilliantly like the Pride of Man,
    and sometimes gleaming it would be,

    gorgeously orange in any late afternoon sun,
or if foggy and only tower tops visible in pillowy white,
    then a reminder to us of that day near 30 years ago,
    Uncle Tom the Child Killer circling above the fog,
        my mother and him crowded in that tandem Cub,
        HP in her belly squirming and writhing to come forth,
        mamma reaching back over her shoulder for Uncle Tom's hand,
            their hearts in their throats,
            life and death in the fog below them,
    and down into that fog Uncle Tom skidded that Cub,
        totally on instincts and a stranger's advice,
        using the Bridge tower as his outer marker,
        not seeing the runway until 30 feet above it,
    and then as he had done so many times before
        during the war in his B-17 Bomber,
he landed that plane safely and easily,
    only this time landing on Chrissy Field,
        a minute's ride to the Presidio and Letterman's Hospital,
            and HP saved who now hugged me tight over the Bridge,
        and 20 years passed before we knew the whole story of it,
        and 5 years after that the two of us there on that Harley...

Epilogue

During that entire sickle ride, me and HP,
    because of our helmets and earplugs,
we never spoke more than 100 words,
    except of course stopped for gas
    her standing there beside Avatar the Sickle,
    rubbing sunscreen on her face carefully.

Otherwise it was all arms around me, the whole time,
    her breasts pressed up against me,
    hankie and credit card nestled between them,
        just rolling with me in her state of perfect trust,
        and eventually her howling like a running she-wolf.

This all of course would be some years in the future
    from that evening at the restaurant with Peying and Wilson,
and well after Spain and Sniperville for me,
    and for her after assuming sole leadership of the Barbary Coast Theater
when she tried to maintain 2 separate relationships,
    and each of those in her 2 separate worlds,

one world with a son of light and color,
    now become a Silkie from the sea,
and in the other a mesmerizing Count Cagliostro, the Kraken,
    up and upon her out of the Heart of Darkness,
        and her so mesmerized she could not see it,
            nor trust my vision and Marine instincts about him,
                as she had trusted me so thoroughly that day on our rolling ecstasy,
                    nor anyone else she trusted enough to veer her away from him,
and from such a blind arrogant misadventure,
    trusting that Kraken,
can come only tragedy and horrific experience,
something far deeper than our fatiguing joyfully howling ride,
    through a world of magnificent vision and vibrating bones.

END OF FRAGMENT

The Scarlet Knight Meets The Whore Of Babylon

And Other Tales and Selected Poetry

From the Modern Epic:

THE ADVENTURES OF
HIGHPOCKETS AND THE BLUE GUITAR,
SEARCHING FOR THE FACE OF GOD

Including:

THE JOURNAL OF TARANIS THE HELVETIAN
THE MAN WHO LOVES WILD REDCAT WOMAN,
KAZHANA THE AKATANI

By
JAMES MCMILLAN

The man bent over his guitar…
"We see you have a blue guitar,
but play you must things as they are."
The man replied, "Things as they are
are changed upon the blue guitar."
—W.S.

Author's Note

Originally the title of this work was simply "HighPockets."

But my writing son thought that horrible, just awful.

So then it became "HighPockets, Searching for the Face of God."

No, that was no better, maybe even worse.

After a time I changed it to "The Epic of HighPockets and the Blue Guitar, Searching for the Face of God," with the W.S. quote to explain.

Nope.

I said how about this, "The Scarlet Knight Meets the Whore of Babylon."

He liked that okay.

So I said, Fuck it, and wrote out the entire title as it is now.

He just shrugged and said, Get a grip.

Then I said, you write something as an unknown and get it published.

He's working on that now.

All this just goes to show you that even book titles can have evolution.

JMc

Editor's Preface

Here now see the life and fate of a Renaissance man, out of time.

This is a complex and layered man, so lauded as warrior-poet by some, yet scorned as bloodthirsty vigilante by authorities, and then labeled by print and TV media monolithically as an incestuous racist assassin. Yet always he refers to himself simply as Stevie, to his sister as HighPockets, and to his lifelong friend Mary Madelin as Miss Mary, and he loved to write poetry play piano, sing, and tell jokes. Tell me, does that sound like tragedy or parlor farce?

To really understand the raging controversy over this unclassifiable man demands way more than simply listening to these rhapsodic tapes of his life and times. He recorded these tapes shortly after the chaos at the trial of the now notorious Chilo murders, when a bucket of gangster blood got splattered upon fawning media and terrified them, like bull sharks up their river, as Stevie would say. Now, three years later it truly seems farcical that appearance back then of these several tapes in the San Francisco Chronicle, though poorly edited and highly censored, then turned into a feeding frenzy and sent halfway around the world a shockwave that created outrageous media stampede followed by both praise and carnage of multiple reputations and characters.

As evidenced by Stevie's great smile in his now famous photograph, he himself found that frenzy comical, a knee slapping belly-laugh, way more funny than did Mary Madelin, or his sister, who found themselves huge players throughout these tapes and at those trials (such that Mary calls herself mockingly Stevie's 'Sancha Panza',) Nor, it must be said, are any other of the tapes' living players, from San Francisco to Spain and from Africa to Kuwait, are they at all pleased with their own inclusion in these memoirs. Yet none of those interviewed, neither civilian nor military, sued to block this publication of these tapes, now uncensored, not even the laconic but candid Colonel Mooring, creator of Stevie's black ops sniper unit, known among Marines as the Harlot Moor's, and themselves now become eager topic at dinner tables and student unions, and also, it now seems, have they become inundated by volunteers.

Those who did sue to block us were the Egyptian general, for obvious reasons, and our State Department, for paranoia reasons, and several total unknowns solely for financial reasons, claiming as they did to be blood of the Chilo, all thankfully turned away by American courts. Amazingly the Catholic Church has remained completely aloof and silent, not one word, not even the token pursuit of copyright infringement, which surprised us. Perhaps in the end they felt this work was actually good press for them.

For me, down now comes the curtain on my long involvement with this man Stevie, from pursuing his tapes, to acquiring them, to editing them for clarity in the style I believe he meant for them. I alone interviewed every player possible on these tapes all across the world, only one refusing to see me and contribute, only one. Each spoke unabashedly about Stevie, though certainly not always kindly, and even many times were they out right angry, but still never contradicting his recollections, though several at least faced personal jeopardy and outright danger because of these tapes, and not just those in the Middle East

From me, my own contribution is that to really know this man you must understand yet another man, Taranis, whose very existence is fogged in doubt, Taranis being the ancient character Stevie read about in his youth, the last remaining copy apparently of the 2000-year-old Journal, 'Taranis the Helvetian.' In my view Taranis definitely became to Stevie's mind and consciousness a Secret Sharer and became in his own words, emphatically spoken, "bone for grasp of my muscle and sinew."

Therefore are we publishing this work in a multiple volume structure, alternating the ancient journal with Stevie's tapes. This includes of course the true complete translation of 'Taranis the Helvetian,' the original translation of Monsignor Walsh, which Stevie had read and re-read in his youth, not the remembrance we found in his notebook diaries, which he had written some years later in moral crisis while secluded in Kuwait. Still it is truly remarkable how accurate are those notebooks in Stevie's reproducing the unique translation he had read so many times in his youth, accurate not only in the words but even in the recall of the curious sentence structure of the Monsignor's experimental and very creative style. Accurate as well are the tapes themselves in recalling word for word passages of Stevie's own writings from those old notebooks, written in that style learned from Monsignor, and teaching me now precisely how to edit his tapes listening to his voice.

Also to preface the Taranis volume of this work are we publishing out of context and out of chronological order a lengthy excerpt from late in the tapes, and excerpt about Stevie's own heroes, which includes the late Monsignor Walsh, certainly a beloved mentor. I believe that excerpt to be self-explanatory.

This work as alternating volumes just makes sense to me because several times Stevie speaks of the concept of love he calls so trite it should never need repeating, that we are all one volume in a two-volume set, each of us completed by the other, either by choice or by fate. Therefore it just feels right to me to publish this as alternating volumes.

Even though I did not know him personally, my many hours listening to his unique voice, sometimes whimsical, sometimes lyrical, sometimes rhapsodic, occasionally even singing, but rarely scornful; along with his amazing ability to recall events accurately (as verified by fact checkers) and as well his constant spicing of humor in his recollections (not always successful but still retained)— actually more than spicing, I should say an outright search for humor— all of that gives me a sense of my knowing him intimately. Yet we have never met.

Finally, and this is hard for me to admit, but now when it counts I must in truth confess that throughout my life always have I lived frightened— a mouse and a coward, a bookworm. It is true. Yet Stevie and Taranis, though I be a woman near 40, have become part of me, bone for grasp of my muscle and sinew. I am not the same person who started this project. Sometimes now I catch my reflection in a mirror or window or even on a windshield and I am smiling like he is smiling in that now famous photograph of him on that gurney, with his thumb emphatically up.

Apparently I am still young enough to be impressionable.

Well done, Stevie.
Well done, Taranis.

Dictated September 11, 2003, San Francisco

Merciful are the Ways of God,
Love is the Embrace of God,
and Justice, yes, Justice,
that is the Face of God...

I promise you I will live my life
in righteousness and obedience
so that I will be pleasing
in the eyes of Allah,
and my prayers welcomed in his ear.
I promise you, as long as I have
breath in my body and voice to speak
you will never be forgotten by Allah.
I promise you, Stevie,
God will never forget you...

—Serq, an Egyptian Woman,
Wife of Prince Ali Al-Samarah

Editor's Preface
to
The Second Edition

Life is quick and I will be too.

What follows is the second edition of these tapes, third if you count the very highly abridged and flawed version that ran in the San Francisco Chronicle and started this HighPockets phenomenon around the world that has just about reached Kilroy status.

The first edition was released as soon as legally possible and served to correct and verify and often debunk the pirated and you might say spirited accounts of these tapes that amount to urban legends springing up on the Internet, and also in other venues and locales around the Western world, and even into the Middle East.

Still that first edition fanned the spread of this stunning phenomenon and has affected people everywhere, including Internet reported sightings of many of these various living participants in these tapes, altering their lives, legendizing some and vilifying others, and has prompted in my view unnecessary and truly laughable legal and social investigations into these events, mostly by individuals who all just want to get themselves into this phenomenon for self-aggrandizement.

No matter what psycho-babble or psycho-pap is bandied about, no one understands the need for blood-in-the-water frenzy like the OJ trial and Michael Jackson, or for that matter the James Dean and Che Guevara phenomena, or such as this one here where a nickname like "HighPockets" becomes worldwide code, something like "Subway Vigilante," although in this instance for an entirely different purpose.

Perhaps the cause is what Stevie himself says in the tapes, the absolute necessity in the cycling evolution of human consciousness, the absolute need for the sudden appearance and then disappearance of heroes and bad men, and best if they both be the same person.

Lastly, a word on the style as presented in this work that has caused such furious feedback— all I can say in my defense is… such is Stevie. Read his writings and listen to him talk on these tapes and there is no other choice. Or perhaps it is just my way of injecting myself into this phenomenon. Does that make me hero or bad man? Your call.

Dictated New Years Day, 2004, Málaga, Spain.

www.ingramcontent.com/pod-product-compliance
Lightning Source LLC
Chambersburg PA
CBHW071431070526
44578CB00001B/68